MODERN BANKS

BY VICKIE STULB

ISBN: 0-89538-084-6

Published by: L-W Book Sales
P.O. Box 69
Gas City, IN 46933

Please write for our free catalog.

Printed in the U.S.A. by Image Graphics, Paducah, KY

INTRODUCTION

Early banks were made of pottery, gourds, wood, and tin until the cast iron process was discovered. Most of these banks were used by parents to teach children the value of saving and the word "thrift" was imprinted upon many early banks. Banks can now be found composed of many different materials such as silver, iron, tin, wood, glass, vinyl, plastic, paper, wax, and leather, and some banks combine materials in one piece. Some banks are manufactured with double purposes in that once the original contents are used, the empty container is used as a bank, i.e. candy containers and bubble bath containers. Some banks are made for advertising purposes, many times in the shape of a specific product, a favorite character, the shape of an animal, as a gumball machine, or even as the ever familiar "pig". Some manufacturers have produced banks from popular movie, cartoon, fairy tale, and holiday characters as well as notable personalities. These are the banks on which this book will focus.

Since many banks were made by varying manufacturers in different sizes and materials, the intent of this book is to provide a picture along with pertinent data including size, manufacturer, and year when possible. In many instances, similar banks have been produced by different manufacturers which would result in the same description, whereas a picture will easily identify the differences.

This book consists of modern character and character related banks from the author's collection.

A NOTE ABOUT THE AUTHOR

Vickie Stulb grew up in New Jersey and moved to Houston, Texas in the late 1960's. She now resides in Houston with her husband and has two married children in the Houston area. She has her Master's Degree and currently works as a psychotherapist.

Vickie has been collecting banks of all types for almost thirty years and her collection exceeds 4,000 banks. The search for additions to her collection continues. This book has been her dream as it is difficult to find prices on modern banks and it provides another means of showcasing her collection.

TABLE OF CONTENTS

DEDICATION

This book is dedicated to my family, especially my husband who has patiently accepted my hobby.

PRICING INFORMATION

Values have been determined by purchase price and comparison shopping. This book reflects pricing in the author's market and these values may vary according to geographical area. Pricing in this volume reflects banks in excellent to mint condition, and any decrease in condition will affect the price. Items that were produced in limited editions as well as desire for an item will also affect the price.

The current values in this book should only be used as a guide. They are not intended to set prices, which may vary from one region to another. Auction prices as well as dealer prices vary greatly and are affected by condition as well as demand. The publisher nor the author assumes responsibility for any losses or gains that might be incurred as a result of consulting this guide.

ADMIRAL APPLIANCE
Vinyl - 7" tall
China
$25.00

BIG BOY RESTAURANTS (left to right)

Big Boy with Burger
Vinyl - 8 1/2" tall
$35.00

Slender Big Boy
Vinyl - 9" tall
Marriott Corp. - 1973
$25.00

Fat Big Boy
Vinyl - 8 1/2" tall
$25.00

BORDEN'S ELSIE THE COW
Vinyl - 9 1/2" tall
Borden Co.
$100.00

BOSCO BEAR
Glass & Plastic - 8" tall
Bosco
$40.00

BROWNIE GOLD
Ceramic - 7" tall
Brownie Co.
$55.00

BUDWEISER (left to right)
Spuds McKenzie
Plastic - 16 1/2" tall
A. Renzi Corp. - 1988
$25.00
Spuds McKenzie on Raft
Vinyl - 6" tall
Small World Import Corp. - 1987
$25.00

CHUCK E. CHEESE (left to right)

Droopy Eyed Chuck E. Cheese
Plaster - 8 1/2" tall
$15.00
Waving Chuck E. Cheese
Vinyl - 6" tall
Showbiz Pizza - 1993
$10.00
Winking Chuck E. Cheese
Vinyl - 6 1/2" tall
$10.00

ADVERTISING CHARACTERS

CHUCK E. CHEESE (left to right)

Chuck E. Cheese Hound Dog
Vinyl - 6"
Two different color variations
$10.00

Swiss Cheese Bank
Ceramic - 5" tall
Pizza Time Theater - 1989
$25.00

COCA COLA BEAR
Hard Vinyl - 9" tall
SPC Inc. - 1995
$20.00

CURAD TAPED CRUSADER
Vinyl - 7 1/2" tall
Promotional Mkt. Corp. - 1975
$50.00

DOW BATHROOM SCRUBBING BUBBLE
Ceramic - 5" tall
China
$30.00

HUMBLE OIL ATTENDANT
Plastic - 5" tall
$60.00

EXXON TIGER
Vinyl - 8" tall
$50.00

(Note: both Humble Oil and Exxon are marketing names under Standard Oil Co. - Humble lasted 1959-1972/ Exxon 1972+)

FLORIDA ORANGE BIRD
Vinyl - 5 1/2" tall
Florida Orange Growers Assoc.
Walt Disney Productions
$30.00

AXELROD (FLYING "A" DOG)
Plastic - 15" long
Union Products Inc.
$200.00

GENERAL MILLS BREAKFAST CEREALS
(left to right)

Cocoa Puffs Sonny Musical Bank
Plastic - 5 1/2" tall
Sutton Place Creations - 1991
$10.00

Cinnamon Toast Crunch Musical Bank
Plastic - 6" tall
Sutton Place Creations - 1988
$15.00

Trix Rabbit Musical Bank
Plastic - 5" tall
Sutton Place Creations - 1990
$10.00

Lucky Charms Leprechaun Musical Bank
Plastic - 5" tall
$10.00

GRANDMA'S COOKIES
Vinyl - 8" tall
Niagara Plastics
$45.00

GREEN GIANT "LITTLE SPROUT"
Ceramic - 8 1/2" tall
Green Giant Co. - 1985
$50.00

HOBO JOE
Vinyl & Plastic - 12" tall
Dakin
$55.00

HUSH PUPPY
Vinyl - 8" tall
$40.00

ADVERTISING CHARACTERS

ICEE BEAR
Vinyl - 8" tall
$40.00

KAY BEE KANGAROO
Vinyl - 10 1/2" tall
China
$50.00

STANDING KEEBLER ELF
Ceramic - 10" tall
$75.00

SITTING KEEBLER ELF
Ceramic - 8 1/2" tall
$50.00

KELLOGG'S FROSTED FLAKES
TONY THE TIGER
Vinyl - 9" tall
$60.00

KENTUCKY FRIED CHICKEN

Orange Colonel Sanders
Plastic - 8" tall
Colt Developments Ltd.- Canada
$25.00
Formal Colonel Sanders
Plastic - 13" tall
Ron Starling Plastics - Canada
$25.00
Colonel Sanders with Bucket
Vinyl - 10" tall
Margardt Corp. - 1972
$30.00

KRAFT CHEESASAURUS REX
Vinyl - 7" tall
Kraft General Foods - 1992
$15.00

ADVERTISING CHARACTERS

MACK TRUCK BULLDOG
Vinyl - 8" tall
Keith Sykal Co.
$50.00

MAGIC CHEF
Vinyl - 7 1/2" tall
Color Variations
Lynch Market Intl.
$20.00 each

McDONALDS RESTAURANTS
(left to right)

Ronald McDonald Bust
Ceramic - 8" tall
Group II Communications - 1993
$60.00

Grimace
Ceramic - 9 1/2" tall
McDonalds Corp. - 1985
$40.00

Sitting Ronald McDonald
Vinyl - 7 1/2" tall
$20.00

ADVERTISING CHARACTERS

MILLERS OUTPOST GENERAL JEANS
Plastic - 8" tall
Millers Outpost - 1978
$50.00

MISHA THE BEAR
Vinyl - 6" tall
Image Factory Sports, Inc. - 1979
$25.00

OSCAR MAYER WEINERMOBILE
Plastic - 4 1/2" tall
First Issue - Was Recalled
$30.00

OSCAR MAYER WEINERMOBILE
Plastic - 4 1/2" tall
$25.00

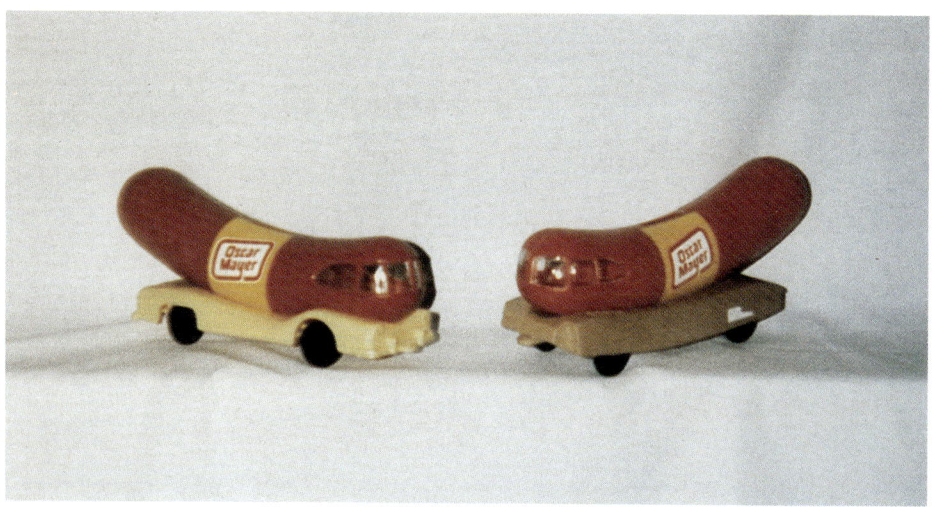

MONOPOLY RICH UNCLE
Ceramic - 6 1/2" tall
OPG - 1985
$40.00

PEPTO BISMOL 24 HOUR BUG
Vinyl - 7" tall
Pepto Bismol - Niagara Plastics
$60.00

PILLSBURY STANDING POPPIN' FRESH
Ceramic - 7" tall
$40.00

PILLSBURY SITTING POPPIN' FRESH
Ceramic - 8 1/2" tall
$40.00

ADVERTISING CHARACTERS

PLANTER'S PEANUTS

Blue Mr. Peanut
Plastic - 8 1/2" tall
$25.00
Two Tone Mr. Peanut
Cast Iron - 5 1/2" tall
$20.00
Mr. Peanut Dispenser
Plastic - 12" tall
The Tarrison Co.
$30.00

CAPTAIN CRUNCH
Vinyl - 7 1/2" tall
Quaker Oats Co.
$50.00

RCA MASCOT NIPPER

Sitting Nipper
Ceramic - 6 1/2" tall
Sarsaparilla
$40.00
Nipper and Gramaphone
Cast Iron - 6" tall
$60.00

SHAKEY'S PIZZA CHEF
Ceramic - 6" tall
$50.00

SHONEY'S BEAR
Vinyl - 8 1/2" tall
Shoney's Inc. - 1993
$20.00

SMOKEY THE BEAR CIRCULAR BANK
Plastic - 4" tall
Old King Cole
$25.00

SMOKEY THE BEAR (left to right)

Standing Smokey the Bear
Vinyl - 14 1/2" tall
Play Pal Plastics - 1972
$50.00

Sitting Smokey the Bear
Ceramic - 5 1/2" tall
Korea
$35.00

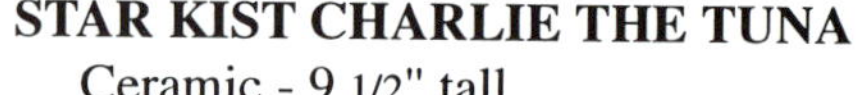

STAR KIST CHARLIE THE TUNA
Ceramic - 9 1/2" tall
Star Kist Foods - 1988
$50.00

CALIFORNIA RAISINS (left to right)

Raisin Cereal Box Bank
Vinyl - 13" tall
$15.00

Sun-Maid Raisins Bank
Vinyl - 7" tall
Calrab - 1987
$25.00

TANG BREAKFAST DRINK
(left to right)

Tang Robot
Plastic - 7 1/2" tall
General Foods
$15.00

Tang Cat
Plastic - 7 1/2" tall
General Foods
$15.00

Tang Panda
Plastic - 7 1/2" tall
General Foods
$15.00

TANG LIPS
Vinyl - 6" tall
General Foods - Applause - 1988
$25.00

TOYS 'R' US GEOFFREY
Vinyl - 10 1/2" tall
$60.00

PATRIOTIC CHARACTERS

STATUE OF LIBERTY
(left to right)

Statue of Liberty on Globe
Metal - 12" tall
$75.00
Statue of Liberty
Plastic - 11" tall
$10.00
Lady Liberty on Marked Base
Plastic - 13" tall
SNP - Chicago
$20.00

UNCLE SAM BUST
Ceramic - 7" tall
Santa Claus Programs
$30.00

STATUE OF LIBERTY
Plastic - 8" tall
$5.00

PATRIOTIC CHARACTERS

MECHANICAL UNCLE SAM
Cast Iron - 11" tall
Sigma
$35.00

MECHANICAL UNCLE SAM
Plastic - 9" tall
Emson, Inc. - 1975
$25.00

DAVY CROCKETT AT ALAMO
Metal - 6" tall
$45.00

U.S.A. ASTRONAUTS (left to right)

NASA Astronaut
Plastic - 9" tall
Charles Productions, Inc.
$30.00

L.B.J. Space Center Astronaut
Plastic - 8" tall
Charles Productions, Inc.
$30.00

PATRIOTIC CHARACTERS

PRESIDENTIAL BUSTS (left to right)

Dwight Eisenhower
Metal - 5 1/2" tall
Banthrico
$35.00

Abraham Lincoln
Metal - 5 1/2" tall
Banthrico
$35.00

George Washington
Metal - 5 1/2" tall
Banthrico
$35.00

John F. Kennedy
Metal - 5 1/2" tall
Banthrico
$35.00

RICHARD NIXON BUST
Ceramic - 9" tall
$35.00

RONALD REAGAN MECHANICAL BANK
Cast Iron - 9 1/2" tall
A. America, Inc.
$35.00

GEORGE WASHINGTON
Plastic - 9" tall
(Winks when money is inserted)
Mag Nif Inc. - 1983
$20.00

LINCOLN BANK
Plastic - 4" tall
$20.00

PATRIOTIC CHARACTERS

MOUNT RUSHMORE
Plastic - 5" tall
$20.00
THOMAS JEFFERSON
Vinyl - 10" tall
Huron
$30.00
BEN FRANKLIN BUST
Plastic - 5 1/2" tall
$10.00
DECLARATION OF INDEPENDENCE
Metal - 3 1/2" tall
American Can Co.
$10.00

CARTER PEANUT
Ceramic - 5 1/2" tall
$30.00

LINCOLN BOTTLE
Glass - 9" tall
Lincoln Foods Inc.
$30.00

THOMAS JEFFERSON BUST
Metal - 5 1/2" tall
Banthrico
$35.00

STANDING GEORGE WASHINGTON
Metal - 6" tall
$25.00

SILVER SANTAS (left to right)

Music Box Santa
Silverplate - 7" tall
Japan
$30.00

Waving Santa
Silverplate - 6" tall
China
$25.00

Red and Silver Santa
Metal - 5 1/2" tall
Leonard - Japan
$20.00

CHRISTMAS BANKS (left to right)

Santa's Boot
Ceramic - 5" tall
$35.00

Santa Driving Train
Ceramic - 4 1/2" tall
Enesco
$20.00

Santa with Angel
Music Box
Silverplate - 6"
$30.00

CHRISTMAS BANKS (left to right)

Short Santa
Ceramic - 4" tall
Taiwan
$10.00

Santa's House
Lights up
Plastic - 5 1/2" tall
Yuletide Concepts - 1984
$40.00

HOLIDAY CHARACTERS

SANTA CLAUS BANKS
(left to right)

Blue Eyed Waving Santa
Plaster - 13" tall
Mexico
$15.00

Have A Merry Santa
Composition - 6" tall
$15.00

SANTA CLAUS BANKS
(left to right)

Christmas Club Santa
Ceramic - 7 1/2" tall
Artmark - 1993
$15.00

Fuzzy Santa
Ceramic - 7" tall
National Potteries - 1954
$50.00

Christmas Fund Santa
Small Lock on Sack
Ceramic - 7" tall
Marked #1449
$50.00

SANTA CLAUS BANKS (left to right)

Mechanical Santa
Cast Iron - 6" tall
Omnibus - Taiwan
$30.00

Human Bean Santa
Ceramic - 5" tall
Enesco - 1981
$35.00

Santa Claus Post Office
Composition - 7" tall
$40.00

SANTA GUMBALL
Plastic - 9" tall
Carousel - Taiwan
$25.00

SANTA DRIVING TRAIN
Ceramic - 6" tall
Enesco - Indonesia - 1992
$20.00

CURLYQUE SANTA
Ceramic - 7 1/2" tall
$15.00

PAINTED HAT SANTA
Ceramic - 6" tall
Taiwan
$15.00

SANTA CANDY CONTAINERS (left to right)

Santa in Chimney
Plastic - 7" tall
Hilco Corp. - 1991
$8.00

Santa Mug
Plastic - 6 1/2" tall
Hilco Corp. - 1990
$8.00

CERAMIC SANTAS (left to right)

Santa Driving Snowmobile
Ceramic - 6" tall
Enesco - Indonesia - 1992
$20.00

Santa Head
Porcelain - 6" tall
China
$15.00

SANTA'S FIRE TRUCK
Ceramic - 5" tall
Enesco - 1991
$20.00

SANTA'S AIRPLANE
Ceramic - 5" tall
Enesco - 1991
$20.00

CERAMIC SANTA CLAUS BANKS (left to right)

Waving Santa
Ceramic - 7 1/2" tall
Japan - 1950's
$55.00

Cowboy Santa
Ceramic - 8" tall
Enesco - 1980's
$25.00

SANTAS CARRYING SACKS (left to right)

Santa with Teddy
Porcelain - 6 1/2" tall
Unmarked
$20.00

Bashful Santa with Sack
Composition - 6" tall
Berrie - 1971
$25.00

SANTAS CARRYING SACKS (left to right)

White Santa
Ceramic - 7 1/2" tall
(Hand hole will bear artificial trees, lollipops, etc.)
Russ Berrie - Taiwan
$20.00

Pastel Santa
Plaster - 7" tall
Enesco - 1989
$20.00

SANTA HOLDING TREE
Plastic - 7" tall
Mitchell Simon
$18.00

BOBBIN HEAD SANTA
Composition - 7" tall
Nasco - Japan - 1960's
$55.00

SANTA WITH TOYS & MONEY
Rubber - 7" tall
Christmas Club - 1972
$20.00

SANTA WITH PIPE & SACK
Porcelain - 7" tall
Enesco
$20.00

SANTA AND MOUSE
Ceramic - 6 1/2" tall
Taiwan
$20.00

BLUE EYED SANTA MUSIC BOX
Ceramic - 6 1/2" tall
China
$25.00

SANTA WITH SMILE
Ceramic - 5" tall
R.O.C. - Taiwan - 1980's
$20.00

SANTA WITH PIPE
(Music Box & Lighted Pipe)
Rubber & Plush - 10" tall
B.O. - Taiwan - 1970's
$30.00

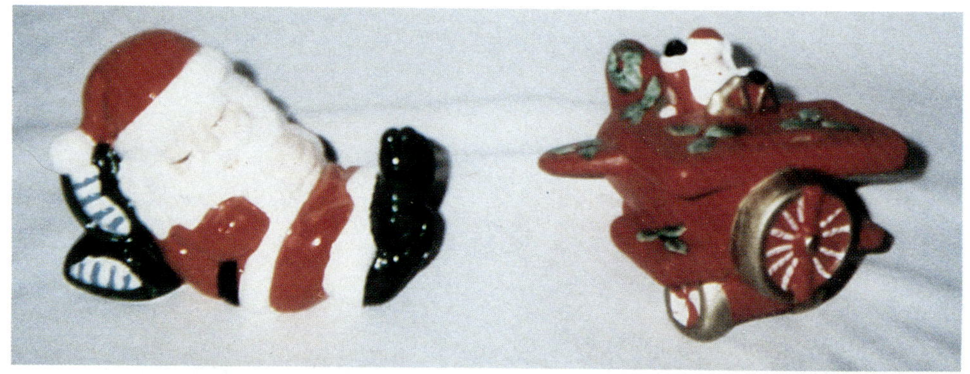

SLEEPING SANTA
Ceramic - 4 1/2" tall
Frankel - Taiwan
$20.00

SANTA'S HOLIDAY PLANE
Ceramic - 4 1/2" tall
China - 1992
$10.00

FULL BEARDED SANTA
Ceramic - 6" tall
Taiwan
$20.00

ROLY POLY SANTA
Ceramic - 6" tall
Taiwan
$20.00

SANTA SLEEPING IN CHAIR
Vinyl - 6 1/2" tall
Banthrico
$30.00

STANDING SNOWMAN
Hard Plastic - 9 1/2" tall
Royalty Industries
$35.00

SNOWMAN WITH STOCKING
Ceramic - 6 1/2" tall
Taiwan
$15.00

SNOWMAN WITH BROOM
Ceramic - 6 1/2" tall
Taiwan
$15.00

HOLIDAY SNOWMEN (left to right)

Black and White Snowman
Ceramic - 7" tall
China
$15.00

Candy Container Snowman
Plastic - 7" tall
Hilco Corp. - 1991
$8.00

BUNNY ON TREE STUMP GUMBALL MACHINE
Plastic - 9" tall
Carousel - 1995
$10.00

BUNNY WITH PINK NOSE MUSIC BOX
Plastic - 4" tall
Topps Co. - 1995
$8.00

BUNNY FLYING AIRPLANE
Porcelain - 6 1/2" tall
$10.00

CHICKEN PULLING EGG HOUSE
Porcelain - 7" tall
$10.00

EGG HOUSES (VARIATIONS)
Porcelain - 6" tall
$5.00 each

BUNNY WITH CHICK
Ceramic - 6" tall
Papel
$10.00

FUNNY BUNNIES (left to right)

TUBE BUNNY
Cardboard - 11" tall
Tootsie Roll
$5.00

HUMAN BEAN BUNNY
Ceramic - 6" tall
Enesco - 1981
$35.00

BUNNY GUMBALL MACHINE
Plastic - 6" tall
Carousel
$10.00

CERAMIC SPOOKS (left to right)

Ghost with Arms Raised
Ceramic - 12" tall
Billies Ceramics - 1970's
$30.00
Ghost with Top Hat
Ceramic - 5" tall
China
$10.00

PLASTIC HALLOWEEN BANKS (left to right)

Pumpkin with Hat
Plastic - 4" tall
China - 1994
$5.00
Dracula
Plastic - 4" tall
China - 1994
$5.00

PLASTIC HALLOWEEN BANKS (left to right)

Ghost with Pumpkin
Plastic - 4" tall
China - 1994
$5.00
Witch with Broom
Plastic - 1994
$5.00

MOVIE CHARACTERS AND CELEBRITIES

E.T. -THE EXTRATERRESTRIAL (two views shown)

Vinyl - 9" tall
Universal Studios
$25.00

E.T. CIRCULAR BANK
Ceramic - 5" tall
$20.00

E.T. BUST
Ceramic - 10" tall
$20.00

E.T. SALUTING
Ceramic - 11" tall
$20.00

GHOSTBUSTERS GUMBALL MACHINE (two variations)
Plastic - 7" tall
Superior Toy Co.
$15.00 each

KING KONG BANKS (left to right)

King Kong on House
Vinyl - 12 1/2" tall
Relic Art - R.K.O. - 1977
$45.00

Standing King Kong
Vinyl - 17" tall
Renzi Corp. - 1963
$65.00

King Kong on Empire State Building
Plastic - 18 1/2" tall
Climbs up and down
T.P.S. - Japan
$75.00

GODZILLA
Vinyl - 7 1/2" tall
movable arms
Trendmasters - 1994
$20.00

PLANET OF THE APES BANKS (left to right)

Dr. Zaius
Plastic - 17" tall
Renzi Corp. - 1967
$40.00

Galen
Vinyl - 11" tall
Play Pal Plastics - 1974
$40.00

Dr. Zaius
Vinyl - 11" tall
Play Pal Plastics - 1967
$40.00

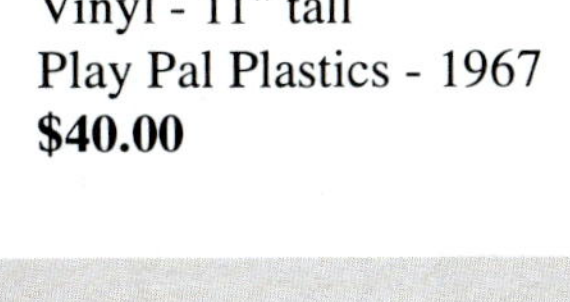

NIGHTMARE BEFORE CHRISTMAS MAYOR (TWO VIEWS)
Ceramic - 8" tall
double faced
Disney - Schmidt
$85.00

STAR WARS REBEL CHARACTERS (left to right)

R2-D2
Ceramic - 8 1/2" tall
20th Century Fox - 1977
$60.00

Yoda
Ceramic - 7 1/2" tall
Sigma
$45.00

Chewbacca
Ceramic - 10" tall
Sigma
$45.00

TALKING R2-D2 AND C3PO
Plastic - 11" tall
moves and speaks dialogue
Thinkway Toys - 1995
$45.00

STAR WARS EMPIRE CHARACTERS (left to right)

Imperial Royal Guard
Plastic - 9" tall
Lucasfilm Ltd. - 1983
$40.00

Darth Vader
Plaster - 14" tall
1980
$15.00

Standing Darth Vader
Vinyl - 9 1/2" tall
Lucasfilm Ltd. - 1983
$40.00

DARTH VADER SAFE
Metal - 7 1/2" tall
West Germany - 1980
$45.00

WICKET PLAYING TAMBOURINE
Vinyl - 6 1/2" tall
Lucasfilm Ltd. - 1983
$20.00

MOVIE CHARACTERS AND CELEBRITIES

STAR WARS CHARACTERS (left to right)

Wicket Playing Drum
　Vinyl - 7" tall
　Lucasfilm Ltd.
　$20.00

R2-D2
　Vinyl - 6 1/2" tall
　Lucasfilm Ltd.
　$20.00

BUZZ LIGHTYEAR (TOY STORY)
　Plastic - 11" tall
　moves and speaks dialogue
　Disney - Thinkway Toys - 1995
　$50.00

HAM (TOY STORY)
　Vinyl - 4" tall
　Disney - Thinkway Toys
　$20.00

FRANKENSTEIN BUST
Vinyl - 6" tall
Universal City Studios - 1988
$30.00

DISAPPEARING DRACULA
Plastic - 7" tall
Tenyo - China
$25.00

WIZARD OF OZ CHARACTERS (left to right)

Tin Man
Ceramic - 7" tall
Enesco - 1988
$75.00

Scarecrow
Ceramic - 7 1/2" tall
Enesco - 1988
$75.00

Cowardly Lion
Ceramic - 6" tall
Enesco - 1988
$75.00

MOVIE CHARACTERS AND CELEBRITIES

HUMPHREY BOGART
Plastic - 9" tall
Mag Nif Inc. - 1985
$50.00

BEATLES
Plastic & Metal - 4" tall
Nems Ent. Ltd. - 1970
$100.00

LAUREL AND HARDY
(left to right)

Oliver Hardy
Vinyl - 14" tall
Play Pal Plastics - 1972
$50.00

Stan Laurel
Vinyl - 14" tall
Play Pal Plastics - 1972
$50.00

MOVIE CHARACTERS AND CELEBRITIES

LAUREL AND HARDY BANKS (left to right)

Stan Laurel with Umbrella
Vinyl - 7 1/2" tall
Play Pal Plastics - 1974
$40.00

Standing Oliver Hardy
Vinyl - 7 1/2" tall
Play Pal Plastics - 1974
$40.00

Laurel and Hardy on Stars (bank set)
Plastic - 6" tall each
L.M.P.C. - Hong Kong
$25.00 each

GROUCHO MARX BUST
Ceramic - 6 1/2" tall
Enesco - 1981
$75.00

W.C. FIELDS
Vinyl - 7 1/2" tall
MGM - David Copperfield
$45.00

MARILYN MONROE
Plastic & Vinyl - 12" tall
battery operated- skirt flies up when money is inserted into bank
$75.00

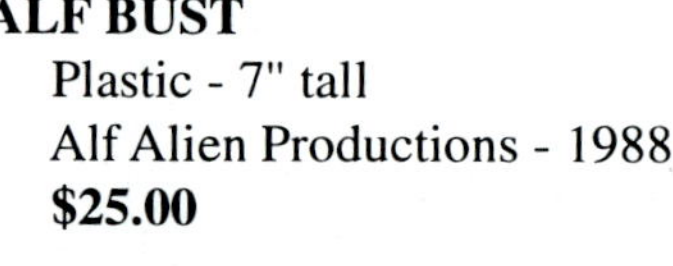

ALF BUST
Plastic - 7" tall
Alf Alien Productions - 1988
$25.00

"DINOSAURS" BABY
Vinyl - 8" tall
China
$15.00

"DUKES OF HAZZARD" GENERAL LEE
Plastic - 5 1/2" tall - 16" long
Warner Bros. - 1981
$45.00

MORK FROM ORK GUMBALL MACHINE
Plastic - 10" tall
Hasbro - 1980
$50.00

BIONIC MAN & WOMAN (left to right)

Six Million Dollar Man
Vinyl - 10 1/2" tall
Animals Plus, Inc. - 1976
$30.00

Bionic Woman
Vinyl - 10" tall
Animals Plus, Inc. - 1976
$30.00

SPACE 1999 BANK
Vinyl - 12" tall
ATV Licensing Ltd.
$40.00

PRIME TIME TELEVISION SHOWS

STAR TREK CONSOLE
Plastic - 8" tall
speaks and flashes
graphics on screen
Thinkway Toys - 1994
$40.00

STAR TREK'S MR. SPOCK
Vinyl - 11 1/2" tall
Play Pal Plastics -
Paramount Pictures - 1975
$40.00

FERENGI
Vinyl - 8" tall
Thinkway Toys - 1993
$20.00

BORG
Vinyl - 8" tall
Thinkway Toys - 1993
$20.00

CHILDREN'S TELEVISION SHOWS

BARNEY AND FRIENDS (left to right)

Santa Barney
Vinyl - 7 1/2" tall
Happiness Express - 1992
$15.00

Baby Bop
Vinyl - 7 1/2" tall
Happiness Express - 1992
$15.00

Reading Barney
Vinyl - 7 1/2" tall
Happiness Express - 1992
$15.00

Waving Barney
Vinyl - 7 1/2" tall
Happiness Express - 1992
$15.00

Baseball Barney
Vinyl - 6 1/2" tall
Happiness Express - 1992
$15.00

DUDLEY DRAGON (2)
Vinyl - each app. 7" tall
Happiness Express
Dragon Tales
$20.00 each

BOZO GUMBALL MACHINE
Plastic - 8 1/2" tall
Hasbro - 1968
$50.00

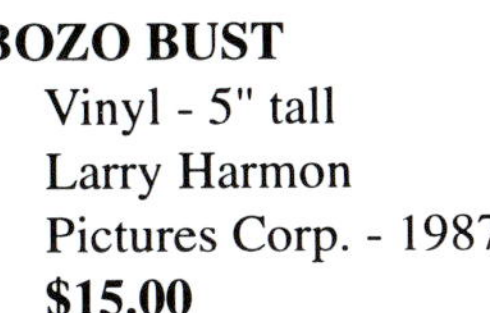

BOZO BUST
Vinyl - 5" tall
Larry Harmon
Pictures Corp. - 1987
$15.00

HOWDY DOODY (left to right)

Howdy Doody on TV
Ceramic - 9 1/2" tall
Vandor - Japan
$45.00

Howdy Doody Bust
Ceramic - 5" tall
Vandor - Japan
$30.00

CHILDREN'S TELEVISION SHOWS

HOWDY DOODY AND FRIENDS (left to right)

Clarabell
Plastic - 9 1/2" tall
Stratco - NBC
$25.00

Howdy Doody
Plastic - 9" tall
Stratco - NBC
$25.00

Mr. Bluster
Plastic - 9 1/2" tall
Stratco - NBC
$25.00

MIGHTY MORPHIN' POWER RANGERS (left to right)

Red Ranger
Plastic - 7" tall
Happiness Express - 1994
$15.00

King Sphinx
Vinyl - 7" tall
Happiness Express - 1994
$15.00

Megazord
Vinyl - 7" tall
Happiness Express - 1994
$15.00

Yellow Ranger
Plastic - 7" tall
Happiness Express - 1994
$15.00

POWER RANGERS PUZZLE CAN
Plastic - 4 1/2" tall
Saban - 1994
$15.00

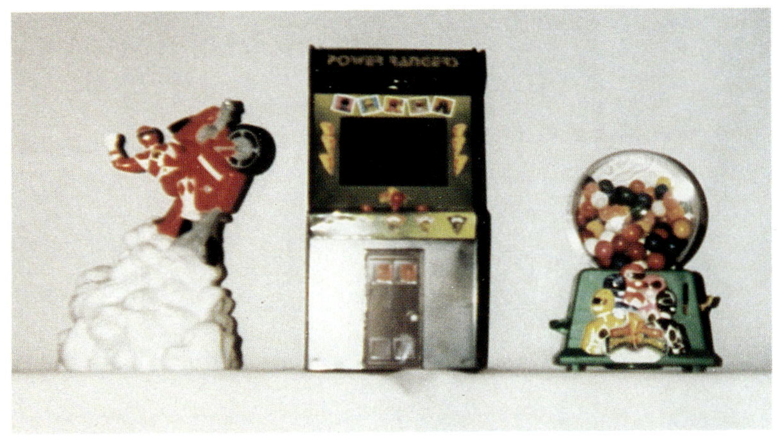

MIGHTY MORPHIN' POWER RANGERS (left to right)

Red Ranger on Motorcycle
Plastic - 8 1/2" tall
Happiness Express - 1994
$15.00

Power Ranger Arcade
Plastic - 10" tall
shows graphics
plays music
Happiness Express - 1994
$35.00

Power Ranger Gumball Machine
Plastic - 7" tall
Happiness Express - 1994
$15.00

"ROMPER ROOM'S" MR. DOO BEE
Vinyl - 5 1/2" tall
$40.00

SESAME STREET GENERAL STORE
Ceramic - 6" tall
Jim Henson Prod.
$40.00

ELMO BUST
Ceramic - 5 1/2" tall
Enesco - Jim Henson Prod. - 1994
$25.00

BIG BIRD MYSTERY BANK
Plastic - 11" tall
Ideal Inc. - 1986
$20.00

BIG BIRD WITH EGG
Composition - 5 1/2" tall
Gorham
$25.00

JIM HENSON'S MUPPET CHARACTERS (left to right)

Cookie Monster
Vinyl - 10 1/2" tall
Illco - Muppets Inc.
$25.00

Chef Cookie Monster
Vinyl - 9" tall
CBS Toys - 1984
$25.00

Miss Piggy
Ceramic - 8" tall
Sigma - Henson Assoc.
$55.00

Baby Ernie
Vinyl - 6 1/2" tall
Illco - Jim Henson Prod.
$15.00

CHILDREN'S TELEVISION SHOWS

ERNIE DRIVING CAR
Porcelain
Muppets, Inc.
$20.00

ERNIE WITH BASEBALL
Composition - 5 1/2" tall
Gorham
$20.00

SESAME STREET CHARACTERS (left to right)

Big Bird Train
Porcelain - 6" tall
Muppets, Inc.
$25.00

Big Bird Car
Ceramic - 5 1/2" tall
Muppets, Inc.
$25.00

Oscar the Grouch
Composition - 6" tall
Gorham
$25.00

Cookie Monster Car
Composition - 6 1/2" tall
Muppets, Inc.
$25.00

CHILDREN'S TELEVISION SHOWS

SESAME STREET CHARACTERS (left to right)

Ernie & Train
Ceramic - 6 1/2" tall
Henson Prod. - Applause
$30.00

Cookie Monster in Cookie Pile
Ceramic - 6" tall
Henson Prod. - Applause
$30.00

Grover & Airplane
Ceramic - 5" tall
Muppets Inc.
$25.00

BABY MUPPET CHARACTERS (left to right)

Baby Bert
Vinyl - 11" tall
Illco - Henson Prod.
$20.00

Baby Ernie
Vinyl - 10" tall
Illco - Henson Prod.
$20.00

Baby Big Bird
Vinyl - 10" tall
Illco - Henson Prod.
$20.00

Baby Cookie Monster
Vinyl - 9" tall
Illco - Henson Prod.
$20.00

Baby Pirate Kermit
Vinyl - 10" tall
Illco - Henson Prod. - 1989
$20.00

BABY MUPPET CHARACTERS (left to right)

Baby Big Bird with Rattle
Vinyl - 7" tall
Illco - Henson Prod.
$15.00

Baby Bert with Towel
Vinyl - 7 1/2" tall
Illco - Henson Prod.
$15.00

Baby Cookie Monster with Bottle
Vinyl - 7" tall
Illco - Henson Prod.
$15.00

BIG BIRD IN BASKET
Vinyl - 10" tall
Illco - Henson Prod.
$20.00

OSCAR THE GROUCH IN GARBAGE CAN
Vinyl - 9 1/2" tall
Illco - Henson Prod.
$20.00

CHILDREN'S TELEVISION SHOWS

MISS PIGGY BANKS (left to right)

Miss Piggy with Piglets
Vinyl - 10 1/2" tall
Illco - Henson Assoc. - 1989
$30.00

Miss Piggy Tin
Metal - 4 1/2" tall
Hallmark
$10.00

BABY MUPPETS (left to right)

Miss Piggy on Block
Porcelain - 6 1/2" tall
Henson Assoc. - Enesco - 1983
$40.00

Baby Kermit on Block
Porcelain - 6 1/2" tall
Henson Assoc. - Enesco - 1983
$40.00

SHARI LEWIS' PUPPETS (left to right)

Lambchop
Vinyl - 7 1/2" tall
Happiness Express - 1993
$10.00

Charley Horse
Vinyl - 8 1/2" tall
Happiness Express - 1993
$10.00

BATMAN BUST WITH PAPER FACE
Plastic - 7" tall
D.C. Comics
$10.00

STANDING BATMAN
Ceramic - 6" tall
National Periodical Pub. - 1966
$60.00

BATMAN BUST
Plastic - 7" tall
D.C. Comics - 1992
$10.00

BATMAN ON CLOUD
Vinyl - 9 1/2" tall
D.C. Comics - 1991
$15.00

BATMAN & ROBIN GUMBALL
Glass & Metal - 15" tall
D.C. Comics - 1995
$40.00

BATMAN ON BASE
Vinyl - 8 1/2" tall
D.C. Comics
$15.00

CROUCHING BATMAN
Hard Vinyl - 7 1/2" tall
$35.00

BATMAN GUMBALL MACHINE
Plastic - 9 1/2" tall
Talking
$30.00

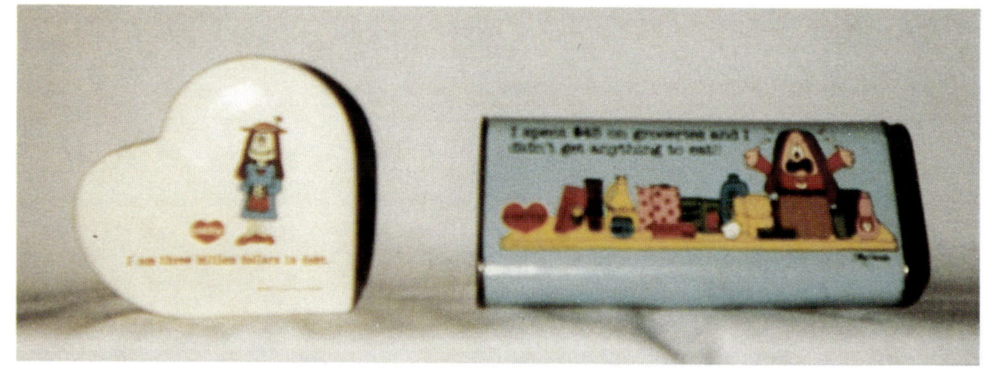

CATHY HEART
Ceramic - 4" tall
Univ. Press Syndicate - 1983
$20.00

CATHY BANK
Cardboard - 7" tall
Univ. Press Syndicate - 1982
$20.00

DENNIS THE MENACE AND RUFF
Ceramic - 6 1/2" tall
1978
$45.00

GARFIELD "DONATIONS ACCEPTED"
Ceramic - 6" tall
U.F.S. - Enesco - 1981
$30.00

TOOTHY GRIN GARFIELD
Ceramic - 5" tall
U.F.S. - Enesco - 1981
$30.00

GARFIELD "FEED THE KITTY"
Ceramic - 6" tall
U.F.S. - Enesco - 1981
$30.00

FOOTBALL GARFIELD
Ceramic - 6" tall
U.F.S. - Enesco - 1981
$30.00

SOCCER GARFIELD
Ceramic - 6" tall
U.F.S. - Enesco - 1981
$30.00

BASKETBALL GARFIELD
Ceramic - 6" tall
U.F.S. - Enesco - 1981
$30.00

GARFIELD FOOD CONTAINER/ BANK
Plastic - 13" tall
Alpo - 1994
$15.00

COCONUT GARFIELD
Coconut - 11 1/2" tall
$10.00

PLUSH GARFIELD
U.F.S. - Dakin - 1981
$45.00

GARFIELD WITH NFL HELMET (various)
Vinyl - 5" tall
NFL officially licensed
$15.00 each

DIRECTOR'S CHAIR GARFIELD GUMBALL MACHINE
Metal & Plastic - 14" tall
Superior Toy Co.
$60.00

GARFIELD WITH NFL HELMET (various)
Vinyl - 5" tall
NFL officially licensed
$15.00 each

BABY GARFIELD WITH TEDDY
Vinyl - 6 1/2" tall
U.F.S. - 1981
$20.00

GRADUATE GARFIELD
Vinyl - 7" tall
U.F.S. - Enesco - 1981
$20.00

"U.S. ACRES" ORSON
Ceramic - 6" tall
U.F.S. - Enesco
$25.00

GARFIELD GRADUATE WITH BLACK TASSEL
Ceramic - 7" tall
U.F.S. - Enesco - 1981
$30.00

GARFIELD ON POT OF GOLD
Ceramic - 8" tall
U.F.S. - Enesco - 1981
$30.00

GARFIELD IN SANTA HAT
Ceramic - 7" tall
U.F.S. - Enesco - 1981
$40.00

COMIC STRIP AND COMIC BOOK CHARACTERS

GARFIELD GUMBALL MACHINES (various)
Plastic - 6 1/2" tall
variation of quote on label
Superior Toy Co.
$15.00 each

GARFIELD COMIC CHARACTERS (left to right)

Odie
Vinyl - 8 1/2" tall
Kats Meow - U.F.S.
$20.00
Garfield Candy Container
Glass - 8" tall
U.F.S. - 1978
$20.00
Baseball Garfield
Ceramic - 6" tall
Enesco - 1981
$30.00

INCREDIBLE HULK BANKS (left to right)

Hulk Gumball Machine
Plastic - 11" tall
Hasbro - Marvel Comics - 1980
$40.00
Hulk Bust
Vinyl - 10 1/2" tall
Renzi Corp. - 1978
$45.00

LIL' ABNER CHARACTERS
(left to right)

Daisy Mae
Ceramic - 7 1/2" tall
Capp Ent., Inc. - 1975
$80.00

Lil' Abner
Ceramic - 7 1/2" tall
Capp Ent., Inc. - 1975
$80.00

LITTLE LULU CHARACTERS
(left to right)

Little Lulu with Carriage
Vinyl - 10 1/2" tall - 1973
Play Pal Plastics - Western Pub.
$50.00

Little Lulu by Fire Hydrant
Vinyl - 7 1/2" tall - 1973
Play Pal Plastics - Western Pub.
$35.00

LITTLE ORPHAN ANNIE
(left to right)

Annie & Sandy Gumball Machine
Plastic - 7 1/2" tall
Arrow Industries
$25.00

Sitting Annie & Sandy
Ceramic - 6 1/2" tall
Applause - 1982
$35.00

COMIC STRIP AND COMIC BOOK CHARACTERS

MARVIN
Ceramic - 5 1/2" tall
Field Ent. Inc. - Enesco - 1983
$35.00

SNOOPY CAN
Tin - 3" tall
Undetermined
$20.00

SNOOPY IN BATHING SUIT
Rubber - 6" tall
Danara
$15.00

SNOOPY IN PAJAMAS
Rubber - 6" tall
Danara
$15.00

SNOOPY GRADUATE
Rubber - 6" tall
Danara
$15.00

"PEANUTS" SNOOPY BANKS (various)
Composition - each 5" tall
United Features
$12.00 each

SNOOPY EGG BANKS (2)
Plastic - 5 1/2" tall
Whitman Candy - 1996
$8.00

SNOOPY ON APPLE
Ceramic - 4 1/2" tall
United Feature Syndicate
$20.00

SNOOPY DOGHOUSE BANKS (left to right)

Chex Snoopy
Vinyl - 6" tall
United Features
$5.00

Snoopy on Bank Building
Plastic - 6 1/2" tall
United Features
$30.00

Snoopy on Christmas House
Plastic - 6 1/2" tall
U.F.S. - Whitman Candy - 1995
$8.00

Snoopy on Doghouse
Composition - 7 1/2" tall
United Features - 1970
$30.00

"PEANUTS" SNOOPY BANKS (left to right)

Glass Snoopy
6" tall
$15.00

Snoopy with Woodstock on Head
Ceramic - 6" tall
United Features - 1972
$25.00

Sitting Snoopy
Ceramic - 5" tall
United Features
$20.00

SNOOPY COMPOSITION BANKS (left to right)

Snoopy on Doghouse
Composition - 5" tall
United Features
$15.00

Snoopy on Rainbow
Composition - 6" tall
United Features
$15.00

Snoopy on Baseball
Composition - 5" tall
United Features
$15.00

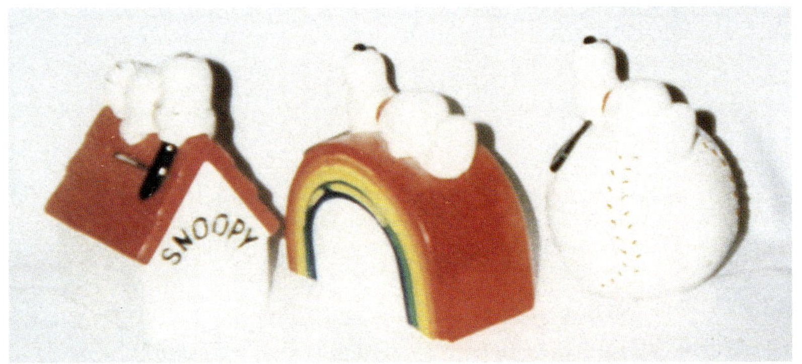

SNOOPY BANKS (left to right)

Snoopy Gumball Machine
Plastic - 6 1/2" tall
Superior Toy Co.
$15.00

Tennis Snoopy
Ceramic - 5" tall
United Features
$15.00

"PEANUTS" WOODSTOCK BANKS (left to right)

Woodstock on Nest Egg
Plastic - 6" tall
Applause - 1972
$20.00

Golden Woodstock
Metal - 6" tall
United Features - 1972
$20.00

Standing Woodstock
Ceramic - 6" tall
United Features - 1972
$20.00

SNOOPY PICTURE FRAME
Glass & Wood - 4" tall
$15.00

PEPPERMINT PATTY
Composition - 7" tall
United Feature Syndicate - 1972
$25.00

PSYCHIATRIST LUCY
Ceramic - 5" tall
United Features
$35.00

FIREDOG SNOOPY
Silverplate - 6 1/2" tall
United Features
$25.00

SPIDER-MAN BANKS (left to right)

Spider-Man Head
Vinyl - 6" tall
Marvel Comics - 1986
$15.00

Spider-Man with Crossed Arms
Plastic - 6 1/2" tall
Street Kids - 1991
$10.00

Spider-Man Gumball Machine
Plastic - 10" tall
figure turns
Superior Toy Co.
$25.00

Spider-Man Bust
Plastic - 15 1/2" tall
Marvel Comics - 1978
$35.00

SUPERMAN BANKS (left to right)

Superman Bust
Ceramic - 6" tall
$50.00

Superman Phone Booth
Plastic - 7" tall
Fossil
$50.00

Superman with Crossed Arms
Plastic - 8 1/2" tall
D.C. Comics - 1974
$60.00

WOLVERINE
Vinyl - 7" tall
Marvel Comics - 1991
$25.00

ZIGGY EGG BANKS (2)
Ceramic - each 3" tall
Universal Press Syndicate - 1982
$15.00

ZIGGY BANKS (left to right)

"For Safe Keeping"
Ceramic - 5 1/2" tall - 1982
Universal Press Syndicate
$25.00

Ziggy & Dog on Safe
Ceramic - 5 1/2" tall - 1982
Universal Press Syndicate
$25.00

Ziggy Holding Piggy Bank
Ceramic - 6 1/2" tall - 1981
Universal Press Syndicate
$30.00

CARTOON CHARACTERS

ALVIN THE CHIPMUNK
Vinyl - 9 1/2" tall
Bagdasarian Prod. - 1984
$25.00

BIKER MICE FROM MARS ARCADE BANK
Plastic - 9 1/2" tall
Happiness Express - 1994
$15.00

BIKER MICE FROM MARS BANK
Vinyl - 5 1/2" tall
Happiness Express - 1993
$15.00

CASPER THE FRIENDLY GHOST
Vinyl - 13" tall
glows in the dark
Transogram
$90.00

FELIX THE CAT (left to right)

Felix Sitting
Ceramic - 6" tall
Applause - 1989
$40.00
Felix Standing
Ceramic - 7 1/2" tall
Applause - 1989
$40.00

FERN GULLY GUMBALL MACHINE
Plastic - 6 1/2" tall
Processed Plastics Co.
$15.00

"GARGOYLES" GOLIATH
Plastic - 10 1/2" tall
moves and speaks dialogue
Disney - Thinkway Toys - 1995
$40.00

G.I. JOE GUMBALL MACHINE
Plastic - 6 1/2" tall
Superior Toy Co., Inc.
$30.00

HEATHCLIFF BANK
Vinyl - 11 1/2" tall
McNaught Syndicate, Inc. - 1982
$30.00

MASTERS OF THE UNIVERSE (left to right)

Skeletor Bust
Plastic - 6" tall
Mattel - 1984
$15.00

Masters of the Universe Gumball Machine
Plastic - 6 1/2" tall
Arrow Industries
$15.00

Princess of Power
Plastic - 6" tall
Mattel - 1986
$15.00

He-Man
Plastic - 6" tall
Mattel - 1984
$15.00

MR. T BUST
Plastic - 11" tall
Ruby Spears Ent. - 1983
$35.00

PINK PANTHER WITH PIGGY BANK
Ceramic - 6" tall
United Artists - 1981
$75.00

POPEYE GUMBALL MACHINE
Plastic - 8 1/2" tall
missing pipe
Hasbro - 1968
$50.00

POPEYE WITH LIFE PRESERVER
Cast Iron - 7" tall
$45.00

POPEYE HEAD GUMBALL MACHINE
Plastic - 8 1/2" tall
Hasbro - 1968
$50.00

POPEYE CHARACTER BANKS (left to right)

Popeye Head
Vinyl - 7" tall
King Features Inc. - 1991
$20.00

Jeep in Money Bag
Vinyl - 11 1/2" tall
Play Pal Plastics - 1971
$50.00

Popeye with Sack
Vinyl - 6 1/2" tall
King Features Syndicate
$15.00

Popeye Bust
Vinyl - 6" tall
BBI Toys - 1986
King Features Syndicate
$20.00

POPEYE DIME BANK
Metal - 2 1/2" tall
King Features Syndicate
$65.00

BART SIMPSON TREASURE CHEST
Metal - 4" tall
Nestle Chocolate - 1992
$10.00

BART SIMPSON
(left to right)

Bart Bank
Plastic - 12" tall
20th Century Fox
Butterfinger - 1990
$10.00

Sitting Bart Simpson
Rubber - 7" tall
$8.00

Standing Bart (2)
Vinyl - 8" tall
color variations
20th Century Fox - 1990
$12.00 each

SMURF BANKS (left to right)

Smurf Driving Car
Plaster - 5" tall
$15.00

Smurf with Hands Crossed
Plastic - 11" tall
Rwenzi - 1982
$20.00

Smurf with Hand on Heart
Ceramic - 9" tall
$15.00

Smurf House
Porcelain - 5" tall
Wallace Berrie - 1982
$25.00

TEENAGE MUTANT NINJA TURTLES GUMBALL MACHINE
Plastic - 7" tall - talks
China
$35.00

TEENAGE MUTANT NINJA TURTLES BANK
Plastic - 11" tall
$10.00

"THUNDERCATS" LION-O
Vinyl - 6" tall
Lorimar Telepictures Corp. - 1986
$15.00

WOODY WOODPECKER
Ceramic - 6 1/2" tall
Walter Lantz Prod. - Applause
$20.00

MINNIE MOUSE (left to right)

Minnie Mouse in Car
Ceramic
Mickey & Co. - Enesco
$35.00
Minnie Mouse Waving
Vinyl - 6 1/2" tall
WDP
$20.00

MINNIE MOUSE (left to right)

Minnie Gumball Machine
Plastic - 7" tall
Superior Toy Co.
$15.00
Minnie Mouse in Chair
Vinyl - 6"
Just Toys - 1994
$15.00

MINNIE MOUSE GUMBALL MACHINES (2)
Plastic - 9" tall
variation on paper label
Superior Toy Co.
$15.00

MINNIE MOUSE (left to right)

Minnie with Umbrella
Vinyl - 11" tall
WDP - Illco
$35.00

Minnie with Basket
Vinyl - 9" tall - arm moves
WDP - Animal Toys Plus Inc.
$35.00

MICKEY & MINNIE (left to right)

Minnie Mouse
Glass - 7" tall
Mickey on reverse
Walt Disney Co.
$15.00

Mickey & Minnie Gumball Machine
Plastic - 6" tall
Superior Toy Co.
$25.00

MINNIE MOUSE AT WISHING WELL
Vinyl - 6" tall
$20.00

MICKEY & MINNIE MOUSE (left to right)

Mickey Waving
Cast Iron - 9 1/2" tall
1989
$30.00
Shy Minnie
Cast Iron - 9 1/2" tall
1989
$30.00

MICKEY MOUSE ON SACK
Plastic - 8 1/2" tall
Walt Disney Prod.
$45.00

MICKEY & MINNIE MOUSE (left to right)

Standing Mickey
Plastic - 14" tall
Walt Disney Prod.
$45.00
Standing Minnie
Vinyl - 8 1/2" tall
Banamex - Mexico
$40.00

60th COMMEMORATIVE MICKEY GUMBALL MACHINE
Metal & Plastic - 24" tall
Superior Toy Co.
$100.00

MICKEY MOUSE EARS
Vinyl - 4 1/2" tall
Disney - China
$10.00

GLASS MICKEY
Glass - 7" tall
Walt Disney Prod.
$15.00

TUBE NECK MICKEY MOUSE GUMBALL MACHINE
Plastic - 14" tall
Hasbro - 1968
$50.00

MICKEY MOUSE GUMBALL MACHINES (2)
Plastic - each 8" tall
variant label & base
Superior Toy Co.
$15.00 each

MICKEY MOUSE HOLDING HAT
Silverplate - 5" tall
WDP - Leonard
$35.00

MICKEY MOUSE GUMBALL MACHINES (3)
Plastic - each 9" tall
color variations
Hasbro - 1968
$45.00 each

STANDING MICKEY (2)
Vinyl - each 6 1/2" tall
slight variations
arms move - WDP
$15.00 each

MICKEY & MINNIE SILVERPLATED BANKS
Silverplate - 5" tall
Reed & Barton
$35.00

COWBOY MICKEY ON SAFE
Resin - 7" tall
WDP - 1994
$25.00

MICKEY MOUSE IN CLUB HOUSE
Composition - 7" tall
Walt Disney Prod.
$35.00

MICKEY MOUSE FIGURAL BANKS (left to right)

Sitting Mickey
Ceramic - 8 1/2" tall
Disney - 1994
$35.00

Mickey with Bowtie
Ceramic - 6" tall
$20.00

Drum Major Mickey
Plastic - 6 1/2" tall
$25.00

Mickey Standing Against Wall
Vinyl - 6 1/2" tall
WDP - Play Pal Plastics
$20.00

JACK AND THE BEANSTALK MICKEY MOUSE
Vinyl - 6" tall
Disney
$20.00

BABY MICKEY ON PILLOW
Porcelain - 6" tall
Disney - Goebel U.S.
$75.00

MICKEY & MINNIE MOUSE BUSTS (left to right)

Mickey Bust
Ceramic - 6" tall
Mickey & Co.
Enesco - 1994
$30.00

Minnie Bust
Ceramic - 6" tall
Mickey & Co.
Enesco - 1994
$30.00

Christmas Minnie
Ceramic - 6" tall
Mickey & Co.
Enesco - 1994
$30.00

Christmas Mickey
Ceramic - 6" tall
Mickey & Co.
Enesco - 1994
$30.00

MICKEY MOUSE BUST
Hard Vinyl - 12" tall
WDP - Play Pal Plastics - 1971
$50.00

MICKEY DRIVING RED CAR
Hard Vinyl - 13" tall
WDP - Animal Toys Plus - 1977
$45.00

MICKEY LEANING ON STUMP
Vinyl - 6" tall
WDP - Just Toys - 1994
$15.00

MICKEY WITH BASS DRUM
Vinyl - 7" tall
arm moves
WDP - Animal Toys Plus
$30.00

MICKEY SAFE
Tin - 8" tall
Walt Disney Prod. - 1978
$40.00

MICKEY PUPPET
Plastic - 10 1/2" tall
Nabisco Wheat Puffs - 1966
$75.00

MICKEY MOUSE BANKS (left to right)

Mickey with Bowtie
Vinyl - 9 1/2" tall
arm moves - WDP
$35.00

Club Mickey
Hard Vinyl - 11 1/2" tall
WDP - Play Pal Plastics
$40.00

Mickey with Hand in Pocket
Rubber - 11" tall
WDP - Illco
$30.00

MAGICIAN MICKEY
Plastic - 9" tall
mechanical
Paragon Reiss - 1981
$50.00

MICKEY ROBOT
missing arms & legs
Plastic - mechanical
Wolverine
$30.00

DONALD WITH HANDS ON HIPS
Ceramic - 12" tall
$25.00

DONALD DUCK
Plastic - 11" tall
Carolina Ent. - 1974
$35.00

KNEELING DONALD DUCK
Vinyl - 6 1/2" tall
Disney - China
$15.00

DONALD DUCK LYING DOWN
Silverplate - 5" tall
Reed & Barton
$35.00

DONALD DUCK FIGURAL BANKS (4)
Vinyl - each app. 4" tall
variations in poses
Walt Disney Productions
$15.00 each

DONALD DUCK WITH SACK
Vinyl - 9" tall
WDP - Banamex - Mexico
$40.00

DAISY DUCK HOLDING FLOWERS
Vinyl - 9" tall
WDP - Banamex - Mexico
$40.00

DONALD DUCK FIGURAL BANKS (left to right)

Donald Sitting
Vinyl - 6" tall
WDP - Play Pal Plastics
$25.00

Donald Bust
Hard Vinyl - 12" tall
WDP - Play Pal Plastics
$50.00

Donald Waving
Ceramic - 4" tall
$25.00

Donald & Piggy Bank
Vinyl - 7" tall
moving arm
WDP - Animal Plastics
$35.00

DONALD IN TUGBOAT
Vinyl - 7" tall
Just Toys - 1994
$15.00

DONALD ON VAN
Composition - 5 1/2" tall
Walt Disney Productions
$30.00

DONALD DUCK GUMBALL MACHINES (2)
Plastic - 9" tall
Walt Disney Co. - Superior Plastic Toy Co.
variations of label & base
$15.00

DONALD DUCK FIGURAL BANKS (left to right)

Sitting Donald Duck
Hard Vinyl - 10 1/2" tall
WDP - Play Pal Plastics
$35.00

Donald Puppet
Plastic - 9 1/2" tall
Nabisco - Wheat Puffs - 1966
$75.00

Donald Looking Up
Vinyl - 11" tall
WDP - Illco
$25.00

GOOFY FIGURAL BANKS (left to right)

Goofy Playing Soccer
Plastic - 8" tall
mechanical
Paragon Reiss - 1981
$35.00

Goofy & Globe
Ceramic - 7" tall
Disney
$40.00

Goofy & Camper
Composition - 5" tall
Walt Disney Prod.
$30.00

SCROOGE McDUCK GUMBALL MACHINE
Plastic - 9 1/2" tall
Processed Plastic Co.
$25.00

SCROOGE McDUCK ON MONEYBAG
Vinyl - 6" tall
Disney - China
$25.00

GOOFY BUST
Vinyl - 11" tall
WDP - Play Pal Plastics
$90.00

WALT DISNEY CARTOON CHARACTERS

DISNEY CHARACTERS (left to right)

Benji
  Hard Plastic - 10" tall
  Mulberry Square Prod. - 1977
  $50.00

Big Al
  Composition - 7" tall
  Walt Disney Prod.
  $60.00

DISNEY CHARACTERS (left to right)

"Talespin" Baloo
  Vinyl - 9" tall
  Disney - Happiness Express
  $20.00

Darkwing Duck
  Vinyl - 9" tall
  Disney - Happiness Express
  $20.00

"FIGMENT"- EPCOT CENTER MASCOT
  Vinyl - 7" tall
  WDP - 1982
  $20.00

PLUTO THE DOG FIGURAL BANKS (left to right)

Pluto with Blue Collar
Plaster - 7" tall
WDP - Japan
$20.00

Standing Pluto
Cast Iron - 8" tall
$35.00

Baby Pluto in Ice Skate
Porcelain - 6" tall
Disney - New Arrivals - 1984
$40.00

PLUTO THE DOG FIGURAL BANKS (left to right)

Sitting Pluto
Vinyl - 9" tall
Banamex - Mexico
$40.00

Pluto with Red Doghouse
Plaster - 9" tall
Mexico - 1993
$15.00

Pluto with Green Doghouse
Vinyl - 9" tall
moving paw
Walt Disney Prod.
$35.00

WINNIE THE POOH IN THE HUNNY POT
Ceramic - 10" tall
Disney - China
$35.00

SITTING EEYORE
Vinyl - 6" tall
Disney - China
$10.00

TIGGER WITH TREASURE CHEST
Vinyl - 7" tall
Disney - China
$15.00

WINNIE THE POOH & PIGLET
Vinyl - 6 1/2" tall
Disney - China
$15.00

WINNIE THE POOH (left to right)

Winnie the Pooh with Paw in Hunny Pot
Silverplate - 6" tall
$25.00

Winnie the Pooh Sitting
Ceramic - 7" tall
$20.00

WINNIE & CHRISTOPHER ROBIN IN BATHTUB
Ceramic - 5" tall
Disney - Carpente
$35.00

WINNIE IN CRADLE
Ceramic - 5" tall
Disney - Carpente
$35.00

WINNIE THE POOH & FRIENDS
Ceramic - 3 1/2" tall
Disney - Carpente
$45.00

CLASSIC POOH READING BOOK
Ceramic - 6" tall
Disney - Carpente
$40.00

CLASSIC POOH WITH HUNNY POT
Ceramic - 5 1/2" tall
Disney - Carpente
$40.00

KANGA & ROO
Plastic - 10" tall
Nabisco Wheat Puffs - 1966
$75.00

TIGGER AT TREASURE TREE
Ceramic - 7 1/2" tall
Walt Disney Prod.
$35.00

BABY TIGGER
Vinyl - 6" tall
Disney Co.
$15.00

WINNIE WITH HUNNY POT AT SIDE
Vinyl - 6" tall
Disney Co.
$15.00

WINNIE THE POOH EATING HUNNY
Ceramic - 9" tall
WDP - 1992
$40.00

WINNIE THE POOH SITTING ON HUNNY POTS
Ceramic - 7" tall
WDP - 1992
$25.00

WINNIE & CHRISTOPHER ROBIN ON LOG
Ceramic - 7" tall
Disney - Carpente
$40.00

WINNIE SITTING ON HUNNY POT
Ceramic - 7 1/2" tall
Walt Disney Prod.
$20.00

CHESHIRE CAT
Ceramic - 6" tall
Spencer Gifts - unlicensed
$30.00

LUCIFER CAT
Ceramic - 6" tall
WD Co. - Schmidt
$40.00

THUMPER ON BLOCK
Ceramic - 5" tall
Musical
WDP - Schmidt
$45.00

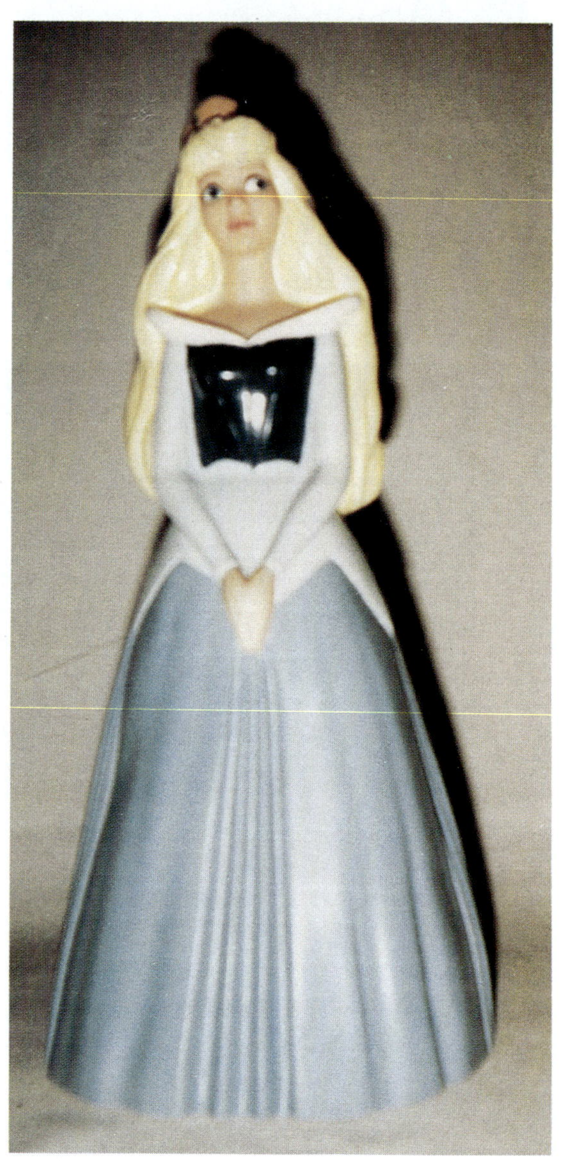

SLEEPING BEAUTY
Vinyl - 14" tall
Disney - China
$25.00

PINOCCHIO ON WHALE
Ceramic - 5" tall
Musical
WDP - Schmidt
$45.00

PINOCCHIO ON BOOKS
Vinyl - 11 1/2" tall
WDP - Play Pal Plastics
$45.00

PINOCCHIO ON PINK BASE
Plastic - 10" tall
unmarked
$15.00

PINOCCHIO ON BLACK CHAIR
Vinyl - 8" tall
Play Pal Plastics
$25.00

PINOCCHIO BUST
Vinyl - 7" tall
WDP - Nat. Bank of Mexico
$40.00

PINOCCHIO ON TREASURE CHEST
Ceramic - 9" tall
Walt Disney Co.
$40.00

PINOCCHIO BUST WITH BLUE BOW TIE
Vinyl - 10" tall
Play Pal Plastics - WDP - 1971
$60.00

DUMBO THE ELEPHANT
Ceramic - 7" tall
Walt Disney Co. - 1989
$45.00

DUMBO
Plaster - 7" tall
Made in Mexico - 1993
$15.00

WALT DISNEY CARTOON CHARACTERS

PETER PAN SKULL CAVE
Vinyl - 11" tall
Disney - China
$25.00

PETER PAN ON TREE STUMP
Vinyl - 6 1/2" tall
Disney - China
$15.00

DOC FROM SNOW WHITE
Plaster - 8 1/2" tall
Mexico
$15.00

SNOW WHITE BY WISHING WELL
Ceramic - 5 1/2" tall
Walt Disney Prod.
$60.00

SNOW WHITE
Vinyl - 8" tall
Disney - China
$15.00

101 DALMATIONS FIGURAL BANKS (left to right)

Mother & Pups
Vinyl - 6 1/2" tall
Disney - China
$15.00

Puppy
Ceramic - 8 1/2" tall
Disney - Taiwan
$25.00

Mom, Dad, & Pup
Vinyl - 6 1/2" tall
Disney - Happiness Express
$15.00

CINDERELLA
Vinyl - 14" tall
Disney - 1993
$25.00

CINDERELLA
Vinyl - 10" tall
Disney - 1993
$15.00

MUFASA & SIMBA ON BASE WITH TREE
Vinyl & Plastic - 15" tall
moves & speaks dialogue
Disney - Thinkway Toys
$30.00

PUMBA & TIMON BY LOG
Vinyl - 7" tall
Disney - China
$25.00

LION KING FIGURAL BANKS (left to right)

Mufasa & Simba
Ceramic - 9" tall
Disney - China
$25.00
Sitting Simba
Vinyl - 8" tall
Disney
$15.00

SIMBA GUMBALL MACHINE
Vinyl - 7" tall
Disney - Just Toys
$15.00

SIMBA IN JUNGLE
Vinyl - 7" tall
Disney - China
$15.00

CLOCK FROM BEAUTY AND THE BEAST
Vinyl - 5 1/2" tall
Disney - China
$15.00

BELLE
Vinyl - 10" tall
Disney - Mattel - 1993
$15.00

BEAST WITH BIRD IN HAND
Vinyl - 10" tall
Walt Disney Co. - 1993
$15.00

MRS. POTTS
Ceramic - 11" tall
Disney
$35.00

CHIP
Ceramic - 7" tall
Disney
$25.00

MRS. POTTS
Vinyl - 6" tall
Disney
$20.00

BEAST LEANING OVER
Vinyl - 10" tall
Disney - Mattel - 1993
$15.00

POCAHONTAS BANKS
(left to right)

Percy on Treasure Chest
Ceramic - 6 1/2" tall
Disney - Enesco
$30.00

Meeko & Percy
Vinyl - 6 1/2" tall
Disney - China
$15.00

POCAHONTAS FIGURAL BANKS
(left to right)

Pocahontas & John Smith
Vinyl - 7 1/2" tall
Disney - China
$15.00

Pocahontas & Meeko
Vinyl - 7 1/2" tall
Disney - China
$15.00

POCAHONTAS FIGURAL BANKS
(left to right)

Meeko Gumball Machine
Plastic - 7" tall
$15.00

Pocahontas & Meeko in Flowers
Vinyl - 9" tall
Disney - Just Toys - 1994
$20.00

POCAHONTAS, MEEKO, & MOTHER WILLOW
Vinyl & Plastic - 15" tall
moves & speaks dialogue
Disney - Thinkway Toys
$30.00

ALLADIN CAT CAVE
Hard Vinyl - 9" tall
Disney - 1993
$30.00

DISNEY'S ALLADIN FIGURAL BANKS (left to right)

Genie Gumball Machine
Plastic & Vinyl - 11" tall
Disney - 1993
$15.00

Abu the Monkey
Ceramic - 7" tall
Disney - 1993
$35.00

Genie Out of Lamp
Ceramic - 8" tall
Disney - 1993
$35.00

Genie on Golden Base
Vinyl - 8" tall
Disney - Mattel - 1993
$20.00

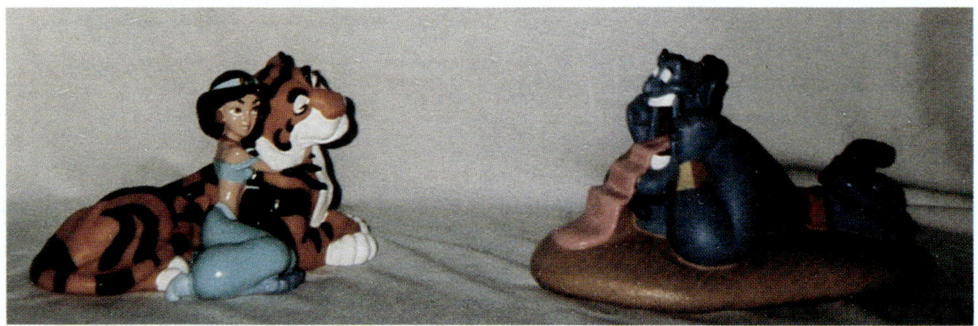

JASMINE & RAJA
Hard Vinyl - 5" tall
Disney - 1993
$20.00

GENIE STICKING OUT TONGUE
Hard Vinyl - 5" tall
Disney - 1993
$20.00

SEBASTIAN
Vinyl - 5" tall
Disney
$15.00

FLOUNDER
Vinyl - 4" tall
Disney - 1991
Happiness Express
$15.00

SEBASTIAN WAVING
Vinyl - 5" tall
Disney - China
$15.00

LITTLE MERMAID TALKING GUMBALL MACHINE
Plastic - 8" tall
Disney - China
$35.00

LITTLE MERMAID ON ROCK
Vinyl - 6 1/2" tall
Disney - China
$15.00

POST CEREAL BOX BANKS (2)
Plastic & Paper - each 7" tall
HBP - Handicraft Co. - 1984
$25.00 each

BRIGHT-EYED DINO
Vinyl - 9" tall
Hanna Barbera Prod. - 1984
$15.00

FRED FLINSTONE BUST GUMBALL MACHINE
Plastic - 9" tall
Hasbro - 1968
$60.00

SMILING PEBBLES
Vinyl - 8" tall
HBP - 1994
$15.00

SMILING BAMM-BAMM
Vinyl - 7 1/2" tall
HBP - 1994
$15.00

FRED BUST
Vinyl - 5 1/2" tall
HBP - Toys Int. - 1988
$15.00

PEBBLES ASLEEP
Hard Vinyl - 9 1/2" tall
Homecraft Prod. - 1973
$40.00

FRED WITH SAFE
Vinyl - 7" tall
Happiness Express Co. - 1992
$15.00

STANDING FRED
Vinyl - 6" tall
HBP - 1980
$20.00

FLINTSTONE BEDROCK BANKS (3)
Metal - each 6 1/2" tall
Hanna Barbera Prod. - 1979
$25.00 each

FLINTSONE BANKS
(left to right)

Fred with Club
Hard Vinyl - 13" tall
Hanna Barbera Prod.
$50.00

Barney & Bamm- Bamm
Hard Vinyl - 13" tall
Hanna Barbera Prod.
$50.00

PEBBLES & DINO
Hard Vinyl - 13" tall
Hanna Barbera Prod.
$50.00

BOWLER BARNEY
Hard Vinyl - 9" tall
Homecraft Prod. - 1973
$40.00

SMILING FRED
Vinyl - 9" tall
Hanna Barbera Prod. - 1994
$15.00

SMILING BARNEY
Vinyl - 6 1/2" tall
Hanna Barbera Prod.
$15.00

FRED IN SACK
Hard Vinyl - 9" tall
Homecraft Products - 1973
$50.00

BASEBALL FRED
Porcelain - 10 1/2" tall
$25.00

FRED & DINO GUMBALL MACHINE
Plastic
Processed Plastic Co.
$15.00

FRED PLAYING GOLF
Hard Vinyl - 8" tall
Homecraft Products - 1973
$40.00

YOGI BEAR BANKS
(left to right)

Yogi Shampoo Bottle
Plastic - 9" tall
Purex Corp.
$45.00

Smiling Yogi
Vinyl - 6" tall
Hanna Barbera Prod. - 1980
$20.00

YOGI BEAR
GUMBALL MACHINE
Plastic - 7" tall
Processed Plastic Co.
$30.00

YOGI BEAR HEAD
GUMBALL MACHINE
Plastic - 8" tall
Sidney A. Tarrison Co.
$60.00

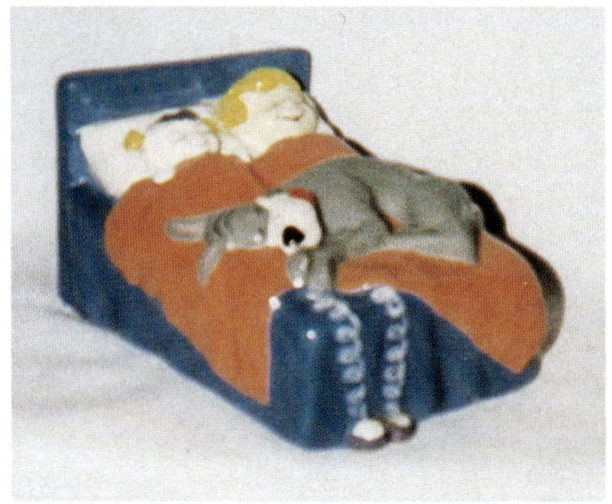

JETSON KIDS WITH ASTRO
Ceramic - 5" tall
Hanna Barbera Prod. - 1986
$50.00

MUTTLEY
Ceramic - 3" tall
$70.00

Huckleberry Hound
Plastic - 10" tall
Unmarked
$30.00

Huckleberry Hound
Plastic - 15 1/2" tall
HBP - Knickerbocker
$45.00

Huckleberry Hound
Vinyl - 5" tall
HBP - 1982
$20.00

SPOUTY THE WHALE SHAMPOO BOTTLE
Plastic - 5" tall
HBP - Purex
$45.00

BABA LOOEY TELEPHONE
Plastic - 7" tall
dial moves & rings
unmarked
$85.00

BABA LOOEY FIGURAL BANKS (2)
Plastic - each 8" tall
variations in color scheme
Hanna Barbera Prod. - 1976
$35.00

HANNA BARBERA CHARACTER BANKS (left to right)

Quick Draw McGraw
Plastic - 10" tall
HBP - Knickerbocker -1960
$35.00

Ricochet Rabbit Shampoo Bottle
Plastic - 11" tall
arm moves
HBP - Purex Corp. - 1964
$85.00

HANNA BARBERA CHARACTER BANKS (left to right)

Mr. Jinx
Shampoo Bottle
Plastic - 10 1/2" tall
HBP - Purex
$35.00

Peter Potamus
Shampoo Bottle
Plastic - 11" tall
HBP - Purex
$45.00

SCOOBY DOO BANKS (left to right)

Scooby Doo Gumball Machine
Plastic - 10" tall
Hasbro - 1968
$50.00

Cross-Eyed Scooby
Vinyl - 5" tall
Hanna Barbera Prod.
$20.00

LOONEY TUNES TALKING BANK
Plastic - 12" tall
$50.00

LOONEY TUNES CIRCULAR BANK
Ceramic - 8" tall
two sided
$35.00

BUGS BUNNY BANKS (left to right)

Bugs Bunny's 50th Birthday
Ceramic - 6 1/2" tall
Applause - 1989
$40.00

Bugs Bunny Gumball Machine
Plastic - 8" tall
Superior Toy Co. - 1988
$15.00

"Uncle Sam" Bugs Bunny
Cast Iron - 10" tall
Warner Bros. - 1994
$45.00

Bugs Bunny Holding Bag of Carrots
Ceramic - 5 1/2" tall
W.B. - Gorham - 1981
$35.00

LOONEY TUNES HOUSE
Resin - 7" tall
Warner Bros. - Gorham - 1994
$25.00

BUGS BUNNY & ELMER FUDD
Plastic - 8" tall
talking
Janex Corp.
$40.00

WILE E. COYOTE GUMBALL MACHINE
Plastic - 8" tall
Processed Plastic Co.
$20.00

BUGS BUNNY GUMBALL MACHINE
Plastic - 9 1/2" tall
Sidney A. Tarrison Co.
$45.00

TASMANIAN DEVIL GUMBALL MACHINE
Plastic - 8" tall
Processed Plastic Co. - 1992
$15.00

WARNER BROTHERS CARTOON CHARACTERS

ROADRUNNER GUMBALL MACHINE
Plastic - 9" tall
missing top feathers
Tarrison Co.
$45.00

BUGS BUNNY GUMBALL MACHINE
Plastic - 8" tall
Processed Plastic Co. - 1988
$15.00

GUMBALL MACHINE WITH BUGS BUNNY
Plastic - 8 1/2" tall
unmarked
$15.00

WARNER BROTHERS CARTOON CHARACTERS (3)
various characters
Hard Vinyl - each app. 13" tall
W.B. - N.Y. Vinyl Prod. - 1972
$45.00 each

TWEETY ON BIRD CAGE
Rubber - 10" tall
W.B. Inc. - Dakin - 1969
$45.00

SPEEDY GONZALES ON CHEESE
Rubber - 10" tall
W.B. Inc. - Dakin - 1971
$45.00

BUGS BUNNY ON CARROT BASKET
Rubber - 12" tall
W.B. Inc. - Dakin - 1971
$45.00

SYLVESTER WAVING
Rubber - 6" tall
arm moves
W.B. Inc. - Dakin
$25.00

SPANISH BIRDS
Vinyl - 7" tall
Serfin
$25.00

SYLVESTER WITH OPEN ARMS
Composition - 6" tall
$20.00

WARNER BROTHERS CARTOON CHARACTERS

DAFFY DUCK IN SAFE
Ceramic - 7" tall
W.B. Inc. - Good Co. - 1989
$45.00

WILE E. COYOTE ON ROCKET
Ceramic - 4 1/2" tall
W.B. Inc. - Good Co. - 1989
$45.00

DAFFY DUCK ON MONEY BAGS
Ceramic - 4 1/2" tall
Warner Bros. - 1995
$30.00

TWEETY ESCAPING SYLVESTER
Vinyl - 6" tall
Warner Bros.
$25.00

SYLVESTER AT THE BIRD CAGE
Ceramic - 6" tall
Warner Bros. - 1994
$30.00

SYLVESTER THE CAT ON TREASURE CHEST
Ceramic - 6" tall
Warner Bros. - 1994
$30.00

TWEETY & SYLVESTER'S JUKEBOX
Ceramic - 5" tall
Warner Bros. - 1994
$25.00

"ANIMANIACS" WAKKO
Ceramic - 9" tall
Warner Bros. - 1995
$25.00

"ANIMANIACS" WATER TOWER
Ceramic - 12 1/2" tall
Warner Bros.
$30.00

PORKY PIG GUMBALL MACHINE
Plastic - 9" tall
Sidney A. Tarrington Co.
$75.00

WILE E. COYOTE
Plastic - 10" tall
Warner Bros. - Dakin - 1971
$40.00

TASMANIAN DEVIL
GUMBALL MACHINE
Metal & Plastic - 15" tall
Superior Toy Co.
$60.00

FOOTBALL TASMANIAN DEVIL
Vinyl - 6 1/2" tall
Warner Bros. - Happiness Express - 1994
$20.00

WARNER BROTHERS CARTOON CHARACTERS

TASMANIAN DEVIL IN BOX
Ceramic - 6" tall
Applause - 1983
$35.00

TASMANIAN DEVIL GUMBALL MACHINE
Plastic - 8" tall
Processed Plastic Co.
$20.00

TASMANIAN DEVIL & PIGGY BANK
Plastic - 5 1/2" tall
Warner Bros. - 1989
$25.00

TASMANIAN DEVIL IN CRATE
Vinyl - 8" tall
Warner Bros. - China
$25.00

BEAKY BUZZARD WITH BARREL
Metal - 5" tall
Moss Mfg. - (late 1930's)
$75.00

ROADRUNNER BY MOUNTAIN
Wile E. Coyote on reverse side
Vinyl - 5 1/2" tall - 1996
Happiness Express - Dutchess of York
$25.00

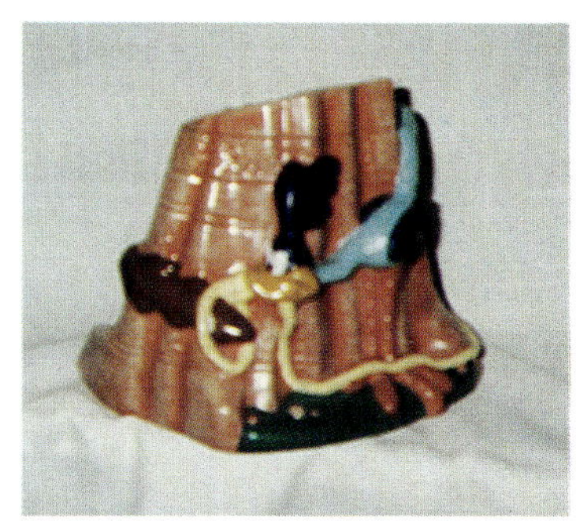

MARVIN THE MARTIAN & SPACESHIP
Resin - 6" tall
W.B. Inc. - 1994
$30.00

BUGS BUNNY & TASMANIAN DEVIL
Resin - 6" tall
Figi Graphics - 1994
$30.00

PORKY PIG CHARACTER BANKS (left to right)

Bashful Porky Pig
Ceramic - 10" tall
Warner Bros. - 1994
$30.00

Porky Pig with Feet Turned In
Cast Iron - 10" tall
$30.00

Porky Pig Holding Coin
Ceramic - 6" tall
Warner Bros. - Gorham - 1981
$40.00

"That's All, Folks"
Ceramic - 8" tall
two sided
W.B. Inc. - Applause - 1989
$40.00

SITTING PADDINGTON BEAR
Flocked Plastic - 6 1/2" tall
Eden Toys, Inc. - 1987
$15.00

CHRISTMAS PADDINGTON
Porcelain - 7" tall
Enesco - 1991
$25.00

SILVER PADDINGTON
Silverplate - 5" tall
$25.00

PADDINGTON MONEY BOX
Metal - 4" tall
Filmfair - 1988
$30.00

SOCCER PADDINGTON
Vinyl - 8" tall
Eden Toys - 1991
$25.00

BASEBALL PADDINGTON
Vinyl - 8" tall
Eden Toys - 1991
$25.00

RAGGEDY ANDY
Ceramic - 8" tall
$20.00

RAGGEDY ANN
Vinyl - 11" tall
Bobbs Merrill Co. - 1972
$45.00

TALKING RAGGEDY ANN & ANDY
Plastic - 8 1/2" tall
Janex Corp. - 1977
$60.00

RAGGEDY ANDY
Vinyl - 10 1/2" tall
Bobbs Merrill Co. - 1972
$45.00

RAGGEDY ANN & ANDY ON BASES (2)
Ceramic - each 5" tall
$15.00 each

SITTING RAGGEDY ANN & ANDY (2)
Vinyl - each 6 1/2" tall
Play Pal Plastics
$20.00 each

BLUE JEAN RAGGEDY ANN
Composition - 10" tall
Japan
$30.00

PINOCCHIO BOOK & BANK
Ceramic Bank - 5" tall
bank stores in vinyl book
$30.00

PETER PAN BOOK & BANK
Ceramic Bank - 5" tall
bank stores in vinyl book
$30.00

LONG JOHN SILVER
Plastic - 4 1/2" tall
$10.00

WOOSTER BEAR
China - 5 1/2" tall
Royal Wooster - 1993
$30.00

CHILDREN'S STORYBOOK CHARACTERS

THOMAS THE TANK ENGINE BANK
China - 3 1/2" tall
Wedgewood - 1992
$35.00

THOMAS THE TANK ENGINE
Vinyl - 4 1/2" tall
Happiness Express - 1992
$14.00

THOMAS THE TANK ENGINE CHAIN/ BANK
Vinyl - 2" tall
Happiness Express - 1992
$8.00

MYRTLE THE TURTLE BANK & RECORD
Plastic - bank 2" tall
Pyro Plastics Corp.
$150.00

TAWNY LION
Vinyl - 10 1/2" tall
Play Pal Plastics - 1972
Western Publishing
$50.00

SNOWMAN BOOK
China - 5" tall
Royal Doulton - 1990
$30.00

JEMIMA PUDDLE DUCK BOOK
China - 5" tall
Royal Albert - 1990
$30.00

CHILDREN'S STORYBOOK CHARACTERS

ILL PETER RABBIT & MOTHER BY BED
Porcelain - 6" tall
F. Warne & Co. - 1994
$50.00

CURIOUS GEORGE CIRCUS WAGON
Tin - 3 1/2" tall
Schylling - 1995
$10.00

BEATRIX POTTER BOOK STACK
Ceramic - 6" tall
Wedgewood
$45.00

PETER RABBIT IN WATERING CAN
Porcelain - 7" tall
F. Warne & Co. - 1994
$40.00

STANDING PETER RABBIT
Silverplate - 7" tall
F. Warne & Co. - Godinger
$35.00

PETER RABBIT WITH SACK OF ONIONS
Porcelain - 7 1/2" tall
F. Warne & Co. - 1994
$40.00

RICHARD SCARRY DRIVE-IN BANK
Ceramic - 5 1/2" tall
Richard Scarry - 1988
$40.00

RICHARD SCARRY BANANA MOBILE
Ceramic - 5" tall
Richard Scarry - 1988
$40.00

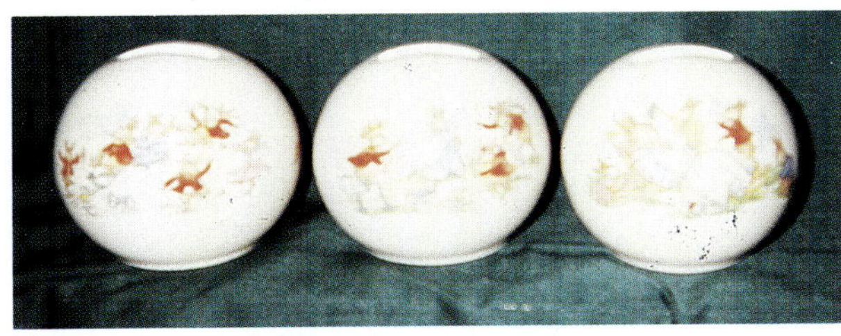

BUNNIKINS MONEY BALLS (18)
Ceramic - each 4" tall
various graphics
Royal Doulton
$25.00 each

LITTLE BO PEEP
Ceramic - 6" tall
Russ
$20.00

CAT AND A FIDDLE
Ceramic - 6" tall
Russ
$20.00

SHOE HOUSE
Pewter - 5" tall
Kirk Steiff Pewter
$75.00

OLD LADY IN A SHOE
Plastic - 6 1/2" tall
Sanitoy, Inc.
$15.00

LITTLE RED RIDING HOOD BOOK AND BANK
Ceramic Bank - 5 1/2" tall
bank stores in vinyl book
JSNY - Japan
$35.00

MOTHER GOOSE
Silverplate - 6 1/2" tall
Oneida
$25.00

MRS. TIGGLY WIGGLY HEXAGONAL BANK
China - 3 1/2" tall
Wedgewood
$30.00

NURSERY RHYME AND FAIRY TALE CHARACTERS

THREE LITTLE PIGS CHARACTER BANKS (left to right)

Mason Pig
Vinyl - 12 1/2" tall
Bankers Systems, Inc.
$45.00

Little Pigs with Wolf
Ceramic - 5" tall
Quon Quon - Japan - 1982
$25.00

FAIRY TALE CHARACTERS (left to right)

Jack & Jill's Well
Ceramic - 5" tall
Quon Quon - Japan - 1983
$25.00

Little Bo Peep
Metal - 5 1/2" tall
$25.00

Three Bears
Metal - 6" tall
$25.00

Three Bears
Ceramic - 5 1/2" tall
Quon Quon - Japan - 1982
$25.00

STRAW HOUSE PIG
Composition - 6" tall
Walt Disney Prod. - Japan
$35.00

NURSERY RHYME AND FAIRY TALE CHARACTERS

HEY DIDDLE DIDDLE
Metal - 6" tall
$20.00

COW JUMPING OVER MOON
Resin - 7" tall
Figi Graphics
$25.00

COW JUMPING OVER MOON
Ceramic - 5 1/2" tall
Quon Quon - Japan - 1983
$25.00

COW ON MOON
Composition - 5 1/2" tall
Lego - Japan
$15.00

HUMPTY DUMPTY WITH CROWN
Vinyl - 7" tall
Happiness Express - 1991
$15.00

BALD HUMPTY DUMPTY
Porcelain - 6 1/2" tall
Dept. 56
$40.00

HUMPTY DUMPTY ON CASTLE WALL
Ceramic - 7 1/2" tall
Omnibus - 1982
$30.00

SLEEPING HUMPTY
Porcelain - 6 1/2" tall
Lillian Vernon
$25.00

SMILING HUMPTY
Papier Mache - 9" tall
Dept. 56
$35.00

HUMPTY DUMPTY ON ROUND WALL
Ceramic - 7 1/2" tall
Markings - 1995
$25.00

HUMPTY DUMPTY HOLDING BELT
Ceramic - 6 1/2" tall
Clay Art - 1993
$25.00

TOP HAT HUMPTY DUMPTY
Ceramic - 5 1/2" tall
$25.00

SUSPENDERS HUMPTY DUMPTY
Ceramic - 6" tall
Avon - 1982
$25.00

HUMPTY DUMPTY FIGURAL BANKS (left to right)

Humpty with Baseball Cap
Silverplate - 6" tall
Oneida - 1994
$25.00

Humpty on Oval Wall
Pewter - 6" tall
Kirk Steiff Pewter
$40.00

Humpty on Short Wall
Silverplate - 4 1/2" tall
$25.00

Colorful Humpty
Cast Iron - 5 1/2" tall
$35.00

YELLOW HAT HUMPTY DUMPTY
Vinyl - 7" tall
Hong Kong
$5.00

BIG SMILE HUMPTY DUMPTY
Ceramic - 6" tall
Russ Berrie
$15.00

BALD HUMPTY DUMPTY
Metal - 5 1/2" tall
$25.00

MISCELLANEOUS CHARACTER BANKS

CABBAGE PATCH GIRL WITH PIG (3)
Vinyl - 7" tall
color variations
Original Appalachian Artworks - 1993
$10.00 each

CABBAGE PATCH DOLL BANKS (3)
Vinyl - each app. 6-8" tall
various poses
Original Appalachian Artworks - 1983
$10.00 each

NEWBORN CABBAGE PATCH DOLL BANKS (2)
Vinyl - each 6" tall
Original Appalachian Artworks - 1983
$10.00 each

MISCELLANEOUS CHARACTER BANKS

COUNTRY BEAR FURSKINS (CABBAGE PATCH DOLLS) (3)
Vinyl - each app. 7" tall
Diamond Toymakers - 1986
$20.00 each

PLAYFUL HEART MONKEY
Ceramic - 6" tall
American Greetings Corp. - 1985
$20.00

SUNSHINE CARE BEAR
Vinyl - 8" tall
China - 1981
$20.00

SECRET CARE BEAR
Ceramic - 6" tall
A.G.C. - 1985
$20.00

BRAVE HEART LION
Ceramic - 6 1/2" tall
A.G.C. - 1985
$20.00

FRIEND CARE BEAR
Ceramic - 5 1/2" tall
A.G.C. - 1984
$20.00

MISCELLANEOUS CHARACTER BANKS

WISH CARE BEAR
Plush - 8" tall
A.G.C. - 1984
$20.00

CARE BEARS HEART
Ceramic - 4" tall
A.G.C. - 1983
$15.00

FUNSHINE CARE BEAR
Ceramic - 5" tall
A.G.C. - 1983
$20.00

SUNSHINE CARE BEAR
Plush - 8" tall
A.G.C. - 1984
$20.00

TENDERHEART CARE BEAR
Plush - 8" tall
A.G.C. - 1984
$20.00

CHEER CARE BEAR
Plush - 8" tall
A.G.C. - 1984
$20.00

MISCELLANEOUS CHARACTER BANKS

POPPLES (left to right) PLUCKY, PENNY, PACKY
Plush - each 10" tall
various names & colors
Those Characters from Cleveland - 1986
$20.00 each

POPPLE IN BAG
Ceramic - 5" tall
American Greetings Corp. - 1986
$20.00

POPPLE WITH CRAYON
Ceramic - 4 1/2" tall
American Greetings Corp. - 1986
$20.00

BOBBING HEAD SHRINER
Composition - 6 1/2" tall
Dee Bee Co. Imports
$125.00

BABY STORK
Plastic - 10 1/2" tall
$45.00

MISCELLANEOUS CHARACTER BANKS

SONIC THE HEDGEHOG ARCADE BANK
Plastic - 10" tall
plays music & graphics
Happiness Express - 1994
$25.00

SONIC THE HEDGEHOG
Vinyl - 7 1/2" tall
Happiness Express - 1993
$15.00

DONKEY KONG FIGURAL BANK
Vinyl - 11" tall
J. Renzi - 1981
$25.00

DONKEY KONG MECHANICAL BANK
Cardboard & Plastic - 10 1/2" tall
$25.00

MISCELLANEOUS CHARACTER BANKS

MARIO BROS.
(MARIO & LUIGI)
Vinyl - 6 1/2" tall
Nintendo - 1988
$20.00

STREET FIGHTER
ARCADE BANK
Plastic - 9 1/2" tall
speaks & plays graphics
Capcom Co. Ltd. - 1993
$30.00

PAC MAN GUMBALL
MACHINE
Plastic - 6" tall
Superior Toy Co.
$20.00

MISCELLANEOUS CHARACTER BANKS

WOOLMA LAMB
(GET ALONG GANG)
Ceramic - 6 1/2" tall
American Greetings Corp. - 1984
$35.00

GET ALONG GANG
CABOOSE
Ceramic - 5 1/2" tall
A.G.C. - 1984
$15.00

GET ALONG GANG
SAVINGS EXPRESS
Ceramic - 6" tall
A.G.C. - 1984
$15.00

MY LITTLE PONY
GUMBALL MACHINE
Plastic - 6 1/2" tall
Hasbro - 1983
$15.00

MY LITTLE PONY
Plastic - 6 1/2" tall
Hasbro - 1983
$15.00

MISCELLANEOUS CHARACTER BANKS

"HELLO KITTY" WITH FLOWER
Ceramic - 5 1/2" tall
Sanrio - 1976
$15.00

"HELLO KITTY" WITH BUNNY
Ceramic - 4" tall
Sanrio
$10.00

STANDING "HELLO KITTY"
Ceramic - 5" tall
Sanrio - 1976
$15.00

"HELLO KITTY" WITH SUITCASE
Ceramic - 8" tall
$15.00

STANDING "HELLO KITTY"
Plastic - 9 1/2" tall
$10.00

THINKING "HELLO KITTY"
Ceramic - 8 1/2" tall
$15.00

PURPLE HAIR TROLL
Vinyl - 9" tall
TNT - China - 1991
$20.00

TROLL GUMBALL MACHINE
Plastic - 7" tall
Processed Plastic Co.
$15.00

YELLOW HAIR TROLL
Vinyl - 11" tall
Street Kids - 1991
$20.00

MISCELLANEOUS CHARACTER BANKS

HUGGA BUNCH CHARACTERS (2)
Vinyl - 8" tall
Hallmark Cards - 1984
$20.00

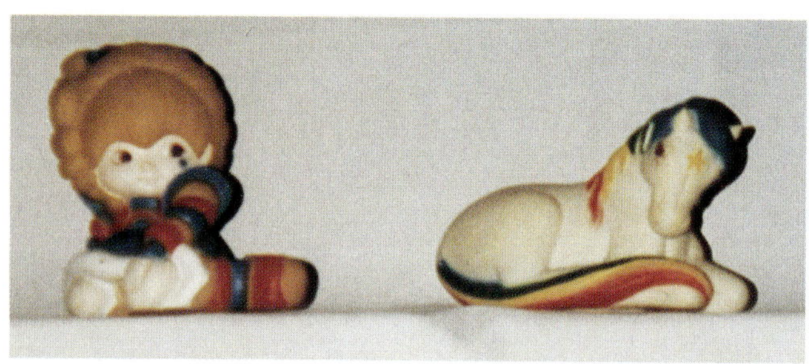

STARBRIGHT BANK
Vinyl - 7" tall
Kats Meow - Hallmark Cards -1983
$20.00

STARBRIGHT PONY
Vinyl - 5" tall
Kats Meow - Hallmark Cards - 1983
$20.00

BARBIE BANK
Vinyl - 7" tall
coin slot under flowers
$45.00

BUDGIE THE HELICOPTER
Vinyl - 5 1/2" tall
Happiness Express
Dutchess of York
$25.00

WRINKLES
Vinyl - 7" tall
Diamond Toy Makers - 1981
$20.00

POUND PUPPIES
(left to right)

Pound Puppy
Gumball Machine
Plastic - 7 1/2" tall
Tonka - 1986
$25.00
Pound Puppy
Plastic - 9" tall
Tonka - 1986
$20.00

McGRUFF WITH SAFE
Ceramic - 7" tall
Sigma - 1983
$50.00

MISCELLANEOUS CHARACTER BANKS

KILBAN CAT
Ceramic - 4 1/2" tall
Sigma
$80.00

GOONY BIRD
Hard Plastic - 13" tall
1970
$50.00

BETTY BOOP CHARACTER BANKS (left to right)

Sitting Betty Boop
Vinyl - 6" tall
China
$15.00

Betty Boop Bust
with Hand on Cheek
Ceramic - 5 1/2" tall
Vandor - 1990
$30.00

Betty Boop on Heart
Wood & Plastic - 16" tall
1993
$20.00

Betty Boop Bust
Ceramic - 5 1/2" tall
Vandor - 1981
$45.00

Winking Betty Boop
Plastic - 8 1/2" tall
Betty winks when
money inserted
$25.00

MISCELLANEOUS CHARACTER BANKS

PIN MONEY PETE
Plastic - 7" tall
Spare Time
$20.00

SILVERPLATE BANKS
(left to right)

Holly Hobby
Silverplate - 6 1/2" tall
Japan
$35.00

Strawberry Shortcake
Silverplate - 6" tall
American Greetings Corp. - 1980
$35.00

LION'S CLUB LION
Metal - 8" tall
ACR Limited
$35.00

TWIN STARS
Ceramic - 4 1/2" tall
Sanrio Co. Ltd. - 1984
$25.00

MISCELLANEOUS CHARACTER BANKS

MADBALLS
Vinyl - 6 1/2" tall
Arco
$15.00

MR. MEN
Vinyl - 6" tall
Bynea Inc. - 1976
$35.00

SHOTGUN RED
Vinyl - 9" tall
Barton Kool Buddies, Inc. - 1991
$25.00

GLOW WORM
Vinyl - 6" tall
Hasbro Inc. - 1986
$25.00

PUZZLE PLACE KIKI & SKYE
Vinyl - 6 1/2" tall
Happiness Express - 1995
$15.00

MISCELLANEOUS CHARACTER BANKS

BEETHOVEN BUST
Ceramic - 7 1/2" tall
Vandor - 1992
$35.00

MONA LISA BUST
Ceramic - 8" tall
Vandor - 1992
$25.00

NOAH'S ARK WITH EMBOSSED ANIMALS
Ceramic - 4 1/2" tall
Treasure Craft
$35.00

MISCELLANEOUS CHARACTER BANKS

NOAH'S ARK
Silverplate - 4 1/2" tall
Gorham
$25.00

NOAH'S ARK WITH LARGE FIGURES
Resin - 7" tall
Figi Graphics - 1993
$35.00

NOAH'S ARK WITH SMALL FIGURES
Resin - 5" tall - musical
Artisian Fair - 1995
$35.00

NOAH'S ARK PHOTOCUBE
Plastic - 4 1/2" tall
holds 4 pictures
China
$25.00

MR. NOAH
Vinyl - 6" tall
$20.00

NOAH'S ARK WITH NOAH
Ceramic - 5 1/2" tall
Young - China
$25.00

NOAH'S ARK FULL OF ANIMALS
Ceramic - 5" tall
hand painted
China
$25.00

NOAH'S ARK
Ceramic - 6 1/2" tall
top opens - musical
MSR Imports
$40.00

MISCELLANEOUS CHARACTER BANKS

SMILEY FACES
(left to right)

Blue Smiley Face
Vinyl - 7 1/2" tall
Vinyl Products Corp. - 1971
$20.00

Yellow Smiley Face
Vinyl - 12" tall
Play Pal Plastics - 1971
$30.00

SMILEY FACE
Vinyl - 6 1/2" tall
Royal Indust. Inc. - 1972
$20.00

SMILEY FACE
Ceramic - 7 1/2" tall
USA
$20.00

SMILEY FACE
Vinyl - 5 1/2" tall
$10.00

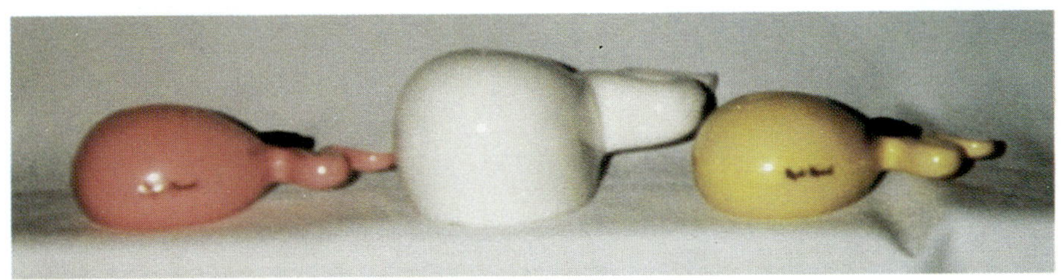

PINK SPERM BANK
Plastic - 2" tall
$10.00

WHITE SPERM BANK
Ceramic - 3" tall
David L. Page - 1981
$25.00

YELLOW SPERM BANK
Plastic - 2" tall
$10.00

MISCELLANEOUS CHARACTER BANKS

MERLIN THE MAGICIAN
Ceramic -7" tall
Clay Art - 1990
$50.00

HULK HOGAN
Hard Plastic - 13" tall
Titan Sports, Inc. - 1990
$25.00

SITTING CHIPPENDALE
Vinyl - 16" tall
Chippendales - 1980
$100.00

STRIPPING CHIPPENDALE
Plastic - 9" tall
dancer strips when
money is inserted
Mag Nif, Inc. - 1983
$45.00

INDEX